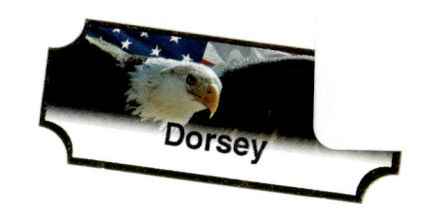

OVERCOMING THE ODDS

To: Jimmy & Louise
Best Wishes

Kenneth Fluellen

Copyright © 2023

Kenneth Fluellen

ISBN: 9798870234496

All Rights Reserved. Any unauthorized reprint or use of this material is strictly prohibited. No part of this book may be reproduced or transmitted in any form or by any means, electronic or mechanical, including photocopying, recording, or by any information storage and retrieval system without express written permission from the author.

All reasonable attempts have been made to verify the accuracy of the information provided in this publication. Nevertheless, the author assumes no responsibility for any errors and/or omissions.

Table of Contents

CHAPTER 1 1

CHAPTER 2 4

CHAPTER 3 16

CHAPTER 4 20

CHAPTER 5 25

CHAPTER 6 28

CHAPTER 7 30

CHAPTER 8 34

CHAPTER 9 37

CHAPTER 10 40

CHAPTER 11 43

CHAPTER 12 45

CHAPTER 13 47

CHAPTER 14 50

CHAPTER 15 54

CHAPTER 16 57

CHAPTER 17 60

CHAPTER 18 67

CHAPTER 19 69

CHAPTER 20 76

CHAPTER 21 85

CHAPTER 22 91

CHAPTER 23 94

CHAPTER 24 98

CHAPTER 25 101

CHAPTER 26 105

CHAPTER 27 112

CHAPTER 28 115

CHAPTER 1

OVERCOMING THE ODDS

Heroes comes in all shapes and sizes. The year was 2009 in Warner Robins, Georgia. The was school Warner Robins High and an athlete playing in his senior year scored 44 points in a basketball game, breaking the school record that had stood for many years and has not been broken so far.

This young man is my hero for many reasons not because he scored 44 points in a game but because of all the odds he overcame to get to this level. To understand how he became my hero we will have to go back many years.

In 1986 as a newly enlisted soldier, I was being assigned to serve in Germany. I was not thrilled about this assignment. In spite of my reluctance, my orders from the US Army stated that would be my duty station for one and a half years of my three-year enlistment. The day before I shipped out my mother did not believe I was going in the Army until the time the Army Recruiter showed up to take me to the bus station to travel to the Military Entrance Processing Station (MEPS) in Atlanta. Until the day I graduated from high school I was always adamant about not joining the military. I had tried college and realized it was not for me. Early in the morning of February 14th I was sworn into the Army and bussed with many recruits heading to basic training at Fort Jackson, South Carolina.

This would turn out to be the most difficult time of my life. Those eight weeks of basic training seemed like an eternity of torture. There were many times when I just wanted to quit. Basic training was already difficult, and it got a lot worse when I was made squadron leader of a group of men. It was even harder because I was the youngest in my squadron and we seemed to have the biggest and meanest men. They had no plans in listening to me or following the instructions that were given to me by the Drill Sergeants to relay to them. Every time their conduct was "not that of a soldier" I was the one that received the punishment. I was so happy when the time came for someone else to serve this position.

My mom was instrumental in helping me complete basic training. At the end of each week I was convinced that I was going to quit. Sunday was the only day we were allowed to call home. My mother must have felt or realized that I was thinking about giving up. She always knew the right words to say to get me motivated and that motivation vanished once Monday morning came and I saw those drill sergeants waiting for me. I was probably the only recruit that gained weight in basic training. I was under weight and several of the soldiers in my platoon were barely making weight loss goals, they were overweight or near their weight limit. They would go to lunch and dinner at the mess hall and get dessert and put it on their tray. Without fail the drill sergeants would catch them and make them give their dessert to me. Needless to say, I was not a favorite of these recruits. Graduation day finally came and my parents attended the graduation I was allowed to go home with them for one day since my home was not too far from Fort Gordon in Augusta Georgia where I would receive Advance Individual Training.

Starting this training on the second week of April, I spoke with the platoon sergeants who had already served in Germany. They told me about the good times they had while serving there and for the first time I started to feel good about going to this assignment. Graduation finally came and I was allowed to spend about thirty days of vacation time before flying to my new duty assignment.

CHAPTER 2

Arriving in the airport in Frankfurt, one of the first things I saw was Germans with signs protesting the arrival of American Troops. The signs said "Go home, we do not want you here." We went from the airport to a reception station where all soldiers coming into the country were received. The majority of the soldiers processing shipped out to their duty stations after about three days. I happened to be one of four soldiers that had extended time at the reception station and it was a week before I would finally ship to where I would be stationed for what I thought would be a year and a half. This place where I was going was so small it could not be seen on a map. I was stationed in a small city called Garlstedt. Who knew that my life was about to change forever?

I was assigned to A battery 4th Battalion 3rd field Artillery Regiment. I became a part of a four-man group that supported a field artillery battery. We supported this unit by providing an important task of communication support If the battery or platoon we were supporting could not communicate with each other they could not perform their jobs. Their tasks were to blow up assigned targets. If they were not able to communicate to get the coordinates and grids, they could not fire their howitzers. Being stationed here was miserable for me. I was going to bed around seven every night. I met a fellow soldier, Rodney Taylor who arrived in Germany about three months before I did. We started talking and going to the mess hall together and to the gym after work each day, eventually becoming friends. I always complained to him about how bored I was. One day he told me that I was going to go crazy, suggesting that I should start going out and enjoying Germany. I was young and this was the first time I was on my own and had money. I also met another soldier, Mark Costello who had arrived a few months earlier as well. We started going going to the clubs every night just to have something to do then I befriended Jaime Santos. The first time I met Jaime in the club he spilled his drink on my shirt. I was angry with him but Mark calmed us both down. Santos and I later became good friends and after about three weeks with my new organization, they all deployed to do training and maneuvers for two weeks leaving me alone in the barracks to continue my required orientations with a few soldiers who were preparing for their new duty stations back in the United States.

About a month after I arrived my arrival there I went to a local nightclub. Germany is well-known for their nightclubs. There was always a German nightclub open in some part of the country. It was this night that my life would change forever. On a Friday night I went to a club in Bremerhaven. I had been there two or three times before and did not think this place was for me the previous times, everyone seemed to be stuck up or thought they were special so I returned to a nightclub called Memories in Bremen, a neighboring city. This club held a lot of memories for a lot of people. I met a guy that had arrived in Garlstedt the same time I did but he also had been stationed there in the late 70s. He pointed out several German ladies that were attending Memories back in the 70s and warned me to stay away from them.

This brought me back to this nightclub in Bremerhaven. I was with two friends, we were just hanging out. My friends were drinking alcohol but I was not, I usually went to the nightclubs and drank a couple of sodas while watching the Germans dance. We thought the way they danced was funny. I walked away from the dance floor after the song ended returning to my usual spot. I was stopped by a German lady, she really was not my type and she grabbed me by the arm saying her friend wanted to talk to me. My friend had seen her friend and said she was cute. I agreed to meet her and we started to follow her but her friend told us to wait in a certain spot and she would bring her over.

Years later I found out why I had to wait for her to come over to me. She was with her boyfriend yet her friend whispered to her that I wanted to meet her. While waiting, some time had passed and I noticed a female bartender staring at me. We exchanged smiles, then I heard a voice saying I thought you wanted me to come over because you wanted to talk to me. There stood an extremely attractive blonde and I did not even notice because the bartender had my attention.

She told me her name was Anke. Her English was decent but who am I to judge? She was speaking English which was her second language and I only spoke one. We spent the next few hours talking. About 4 o'clock in the morning the club was closing, and we were still talking

I asked if I could see her Saturday night and she said she was not sure, stating she will probably not be able to come that night. The first thing that came to my mind was she was probably married and her husband would not let her come.

We parted ways and I did not expect to see her anymore because I was not going to get involved with someone who was married. I later realized that she would turn out to be the one. The next night I returned with my friends to the same club and just as I thought she was not there. Immediately I assumed that I was right about her being married. I did however see her friend that night. She told me that Anke could not make it because she had to work, convincing me to come the next Friday with a promised that Anke would be there. I was a little excited but did not want to show it in case I never saw her again. It seems like that week went by so slow. Finally, Friday arrived and I could hardly wait until the end of the workday. The time had come for us to catch a bus from the base to the city of Bremerhaven where it took us to the American hospital. Several soldiers and I walked up the street and caught a city bus that dropped us off across the street from the club. Germany had a lot of modes of public transportation, one would just have to know which bus to take. I was lucky this night because several of the soldiers that were with me knew the bus schedules and the bus stops. We arrived at Kraftwerks nightclub. The German bouncers were in full force that night. They did not care for American soldiers because they thought we were there to take their ladies and they were right. The bouncers finally let us in. I tried to play it cool because two of my friends that were with me the week before started asking me if I saw her. We walked further into the club and that is when I we saw each other. She walked up to me and gave me a hug. She was with some of her friends so we all hung out. I wanted to know the truth because I did not want to start dating someone who was not honest and was probably married. She confirmed what her friend had told me the previous week, that she had to go to work explaining that she was a baker. The night I met her she skipped work to go out with her friends. She explained she normally had to go to work on Friday night to get all the bakery goods made from scratch and the Saturday morning crew would come in to sell the baked goods. She changed her schedule and we started seeing one another every Friday night through Sunday afternoon and sometimes on Wednesday nights. It was strange to me that after a few months of dating I started to develop feelings for her. I was not going to say anything because I did not want her to think I was weird. After several months of dating my friends started joking that I needed to see other people. My supervisor Sergeant Joel Hardy also started joking that I should start dating other people as well. Unfortunately, I started to listen to my friends and began thinking of ways I could break it off with her.

The time had come for me to go out for my first field training with the new unit. I didn't realize it was a field artillery unit and they spend a lot of time out in the woods doing training. For the first time I had a lot of soldiers depending on me because if I did not set the communications up in time and correctly no one would be able to talk so they would not be able to train doing their jobs by firing rounds down range. I only learned what these soldiers did once they were out in the field training and got to see firsthand how the operation worked.

Initially I thought that the howitzers made a lot of noise and found it exciting. I asked the veteran soldiers how they slept if they had to fire at night. They jokingly answered I would see. They were right, after several days of setting up, breaking down, moving to new locations several times a day and night, I was so exhausted, I had no trouble sleeping. I even slept when they were firing at night. We spent about three weeks in the woods that time. Excited to get back I wondered if Anke and I would still be in a relationship when I returned because there were constant stories of German ladies not being faithful.

We arrived back to the base Saturday afternoon and all I was thinking about was making sure I got to the bank to get money so I could go out that night. We had to clean our vehicles and equipment and take the vehicle to the motor pool before we were released. I asked the soldier working with me to watch our equipment. As I was rushing to the bank, I saw a soldier who was dating Anke's best friend Monika. He saw me and could hardly wait to tell me he had seen Anke was with another guy at the club the previous night. I acted as though I did not believe him but I was disappointed and angry.

I went to my barracks running up to the third floor to make sure none of the supervisors saw me as I wasn't supposed to be there. I was hoping that she would be the one to answer the phone since I don't speak German. When she answered I told her I heard about her being at the club with someone else. She tried to explain, and she pleaded with me to come to the club that night and so we could talk. I decided to go and by the time I arrived there and saw her I had calmed down. She explained that she had danced with this guy twice and she and her friend both told him that she had a boyfriend. Several hours later I went to the bar to get a couple of drinks and he showed up. I walked up behind him, and he asked Anke if I was behind him, she answered yes, and he ran away. This was funny because we both were small guys. He weighed about 127 and I weighed about 128 pounds. The whole night he stayed on the other side of the club keeping an eye on me and I on him. We had dated for several months and I could feel myself falling for her and I believe she was falling for me. I did not want to spend any time with anyone else. No more hanging out with my buddies going from club to club every weekend. I started thinking of all kinds of crazy things people had said about dating foreigners. I thought maybe she was just trying to get a green card so she can go to the United States and possibly move there and abandon me. I started hinting about me going back to the United States. She told me that she was not interested in living in the United States. I explained in that case we will have to break up because I am not interested in living in Germany if I should leave the Army. For the first time she loved me and did not want to break up. I commented I could not be serious about someone who smoke cigarettes or drank alcohol. I was not expecting for her tell me she would give them up to continue our relationship. I now realize that she truly felt the same way I did. We started planning a future together.

My supervisor Sergeant Hardy asked me if I was serious about this young lady and I told him yes, I wasn't interested in anybody else. We started planning to get married and it seems like everyone was against it. I didn't know how her parents would feel about this marriage so I talked to Anke, and she told me if I was serious about marriage, we would have to get an apartment together before we got married. Then she told me that her parents would be against our marriage but if we had our own apartment they could not do anything to stop us. I did not realize the extent of what she was willing to sacrifice to marry me.

My Army unit had a mandatory party for soldiers and their families. By this time word had spread in my unit that we were planning on getting married. A soldier who had been in Germany for several years and was married to a German citizen pulled me aside and asked me if her parents knew we were getting married. I told him not yet and that we were waiting to get our apartment together first so that they could not stop us. He told me to make sure she tells her parents before we got married because if her parents were totally against our marriage they would disown her. He told me that German families were very close and she would not be able to deal with her parents disowning her.

My first winter in Germany, I never seen so much snow in my life. I grew up in Middle Georgia, the deep southern part of the United States and it snowed lightly there about every four or five years, usually never even enough to stick to the ground. I had gone on several two weeks field maneuvers. February 1987 was my first time going on a long field maneuver and this one would last for 60 days in Grafenwöhr. We lived in the woods in tents the entire time doing maneuvers in field of snow. I learned a lot from my Sergeant Hardy, as he watched me get into my sleeping bag with my clothes on, he started laughing, asking me if wanted to be warm the next day. He explained by sleeping in my clothes and wearing them the next day they would never warm up. He told me I should roll my clothes up and put them in my sleeping bag. In doing this, my clothes would be warm when I put them on and they would keep me warm. I followed his instructions and the he was right, I was warm. Those sixty days finally came to end and we returned back to our barracks being much wiser because of Sergeant Hardy's guidance.

I finally got back to spending time with this young lady that had changed my life so much. We continued dating and hanging out every chance we got, planning our future together. Every Friday when we were dismissed, I hurried to my room changed into civilian clothes, grabbed my previously packed bags and headed to the bus stop on the base. At times I departed without my friends because they were goofing off so I left the barracks and went to the bus stop without them. By this time, I knew the bus schedule so I knew if I caught the 4:30 bus that would take me to Bremerhaven. Otherwise, I would have to catch a later bus which would require another stop prior to Bremerhaven. Our routine was we arrived early in Bremerhaven, meet and hang out in the until we thought enough people were already in the club. We did not want to get there too early when it was empty or too late when a lot of people were already there.

After several months of dating Anke finally introduced me to her friends. They acted a little strange as though they did not think we should be together. Years later I would find out that they all had been watching me and telling Anke she should not talk to me because I was a snob. Here I was thinking that the people in this club were snobs, and they were thinking the same about me, imagine that. From this point on we would all meet up together in Krawkwerks, spend a few hours together, and go our separate ways. If we did not spend the weekend together, we would stay in Kraftwerts until it closed and then go to Chicos, a club owned by Americans who came to Germany as soldiers and stayed in there after discharge from the Army. I did not like the club because there were many fights but it beat hanging outside during the wintertime when it was unbearably cold.

Anke and her friends would have to wait for the ferry to go home so I stayed with her and her friends until they departed. It was a river that separated Bremerhaven and Nordenham where they lived. Once they were gone, I would try to catch a bus back to the base, otherwise I'd have a couple of hours for the next one. I usually missed that bus so I would have to catch a cab and that was an expensive cab ride back to my barracks but it was worth it I got to spend more time with Anke.

It was time for my unit to go to the field and do maneuvers again. By this time, we had talked a lot about getting married and getting an apartment before we got married. In April 1987 while we were doing maneuver, I spent a lot of time with my supervisor Sergeant Hardy asking him questions about getting married to a German. Sergeant Hardy had been married to a woman for years who was half American and half German. It seems that he thought my marrying a German citizen was fine. We would make several runs per day to the city to call our loved ones. One particular time when I called Anke she had some exciting news for me, she had found us an apartment and by the time I got back to Garlstedt she would have already moved in. I asked who was going to help her move in and she said her dad and her brother. She explained all I had to do is move my stuff from the barracks to the apartment. I was excited but after I hung up the phone I had serious reservations. Would I be safe living off post with no other Americans nearby? The exercise came to an end and I went to the barracks. After the cleaning of our equipment and vehicles we were released. I got a few things like I always did for the weekend because I did not really know how it was going to work with us living together. The first night was a little strange living in an apartment in a new city. We could hear everything that were was going on outside. All night people were walking and talking outside of apartment. It was a nice one-bedroom apartment but the window in our bedroom was facing the street which enabled us to hear everything. We spent several days unpacking and setting up our apartment and getting to know the city of Bremerhaven better.

When I returned Anke told me that as her brother and father were helping her move, she and her dad had a chance to talk. Several months earlier I told Anke we could not get married unless she told her parents. This came from the advice that I had received from Specialist Jenkins that if her family was against our marriage she could be disowned. Anke was afraid to tell her father, so she told her mother. They were both afraid to tell her father that she was marrying an African-American soldier. Little did they know he already knew. As Anke and her father were driving back and forth, her father asked her if I am African-American. She was afraid and got a lump in her throat, but she said yes. He told her that it would be difficult being in an interracial relationship but if that is what she wanted to do, he would not oppose it.

Meeting the future in-laws.

A few weeks had passed and Anke's parents said they wanted to come over to meet me. I was very nervous because I neither spoke nor understood German. We agreed to meet with them at our apartment. Anke had to interpret everything for me and for them. It turned out not that big of a deal; he was mainly concerned with whether or not I would be able to support her. Once he understood that the military would make sure that I took care of her financially after we were married, he was fine with our decision to wed.

I found out from other soldiers that privates were not supposed to live off base unless they were married so I had to keep it quiet about living in an apartment. If the higher-ranking supervisors knew about my apartment, they would make me move back into the barracks. Sergeant Hardy knew I lived in an apartment and he was fine with it - as long as I didn't get caught. He told me if I was discovered, he was going to deny he had knowledge of my living situation. Specialist Jenkins became a source of information for me about being married overseas to a German and living in the city.

CHAPTER 3

THE ENCOUNTER WITH ALL THE SUPERVISORS

One day Sergeant Hardy sent a soldier to tell me to come to his office. Upon my arrival, Sergeant Hardy told me to go into a room and awaiting me were several other supervisors. I was caught off guard and a little afraid, thinking I was in trouble and was getting ready to be punished. Much to my surprise it was not the reason I was standing before all these supervisors. It had been brought to their attentions that I was planning on getting married. They took turns telling me I should not get married and that I was too young. One Sergeant suggested that I should wait until I was thirty-five. So, I said "With all due respect Sergeant Knowles did you wait until you were thirty-five to get married?" All the supervisors started laughing and he responded that he was in his twenties when he got married. Sergeant Hardy, who I thought had no problem with me getting married, agreed at that time with the supervisors. I was angry with him. Later I realized he was trying to stay on the good side of these supervisors because siding with me could affect his career.

The next encounter was with the senior ranking supervisor. Sergeant Jefferson summoned me to his office. We did not have a good encounter the first time we met so I already had a strike against me. He started by saying a lot of soldiers come to Germany, they want to get to marry

Germans but the marriages do not last. He continued "German ladies are not sincere, they just wanted to marry a soldier to get a green card or an identification card so they can shop on the base." Since he could not convince me not to marry Anke, he stated if he met her, he bet he could convince her not to marry me. I was steaming and thinking I am not going to let him come near my future wife. I did lose control and told First Sergeant Jefferson that he was not my father, and he could not tell me who I can marry or cannot marry. As I look back at this encounter I could have gotten into trouble for that statement. It was clear to me that First Sergeant Jefferson was against African-Americans marrying Germans. I was dismissed and went upstairs to my office and slammed the door to our office. Sergeant Hardy came into the office stating it might be for the best that I do not get married at this time, continuing that we can think about everything for a few months and if we still wanted to get married the supervisors would not have any problem with it.

Specialist Jenkins heard what had happened and told me that the First Sergeant could not stop me from getting married if I really wanted to. He explained the only way the First Sergeant could prevent me from getting married was if I had been punished for disobeying a command and was getting kicked out of the military. He further explained if there was no punishment in my records the First Sergeant could not stop me. I didn't realize when I spoke to the First Sergeant that it was not up to him, and he did not have to sign anything. It was our Company Commander CPT Charest who had to sign the paperwork and his permission was only needed because I was overseas. Specialist Jenkins further explained since I had to enter the First Sergeant's

Office to get to the commander's office, I needed to wait until the First Sergeant was out to get the commander's signature. Several days I waited and watched for the right opportunity. One day the First Sergeant was late coming in and the timing was right. I gained permission to see the Commander, he had heard that I wanted to get married and restated what Specialist Jenkins had told me several days earlier. He asked the First Sergeant's clerk to bring my file into his office, looking them over he saw there were no corrective actions against me, and started signing my paperwork. My First Sergeant walked into his office, saw me, and realized that I had gone over his head. Needless to say, this didn't help our relationship yet I looked at him, smiled and continued to smile as I was leaving. Sergeant Hardy told me that the supervisors had a meeting where the First Sergeant said in front of them all, if Private Fluellen doesn't get married while he is on vacation, I am going to make sure he moves back into this barracks. He had learned that I had an apartment off base. When I got home that day, I told Anke what had happened and she was surprised. I explained to her that when I took vacation, we had to get married if we were serious because of the actions planned by the First Sargeant to make me move if we didn't. We were originally planning on getting married in August so we had to make some changes, we got married in May while I was on leave.

We didn't know how to go about getting married so quickly because it was already the middle of April. Once again, Specialist Jenkins came to my rescue with knowledge on how to make things happen. Jenkins explained it wasn't a good idea to get married in Germany because it was a long process and if we got married there, we would have to fill out an application at the Courthouse. All marriage applications had to be on file and posted for thirty days at the courthouse and if anyone chose to object to our application, we could not get married in Germany. This was the 80's and there were a lot of Germans that still didn't like Americans. More than likely someone would have tried to block us. He explained the best way to get married with the short window was to go to Denmark and get married at the courthouse there. It was also less expensive. I shared this information with Anke, and she agreed to the plan but we did not know how we were going to get there as it was about a four-hour drive.

Reflecting back a few months when we hung out in our favorite nightclub Kraftwerk's in Bremerhaven, strange things started happening. Anke's best friend Monica started receiving roses anonymously at our table. Anke and Monica found out before I did who was sending them and Anke asked me not to get upset because the person sending these gifts was the man that tried to talk to Anke when I was on maneuvers. AJ was no longer interested in Anke, his focus had shifted to Monika. Monika and Anke brought him to our table, leaving us alone to talk. I didn't know if he was secretly trying to get an opportunity to talk to Anke. He affirmed he was only interested in Monika, so we all started hanging out together, and everything seemed to be going well. Now that we decided to get married in Denmark, we needed transportation and AJ volunteered to drive us. He had been there several times and he spoke the language very well. Monika would be standing with Anke and AJ standing with me during the ceremony as my best man.

CHAPTER 4

WEDDING DAY

On the day of the wedding, we were nervous, not knowing how the day would play out. It was an early morning because we had to drive to the border about three hours away and an additional hour to the city of Sonderborg. The ceremony was to take place at 11 am. The four of us left Germany early that morning to make the trek to Denmark, arriving at 10. We were dressed in red and white. It was a beautiful yet short ceremony. We were finally married, and no one could do anything to change that. We had lunch and rushed back to the border. There were rumors that we were supposed to stay in Denmark for 24 hours in order for our marriage to be legal but no one told us that at the courthouse so we made it back to the border and crossed over into Germany. We arrived back at our apartment as man and wife. Not sure what our future would hold, we were just happy to be united in marriage.

My two week vacation came to an end and I returned to work. When I arrived back to the base, I had to process my wife as my dependent, getting her an identification card so she could travel on the base. She had full privileges on all military bases to conduct business she needed as my spouse. Because I was no longer a single soldier, I had to extend my tour in Germany for an additional year and half to become command sponsored so that the Army would ship all my furniture and cars to the United States once I was stationed with a unit in the United States.

Life as a married soldier stationed overseas brought several perks such as an increase in pay to afford our apartment and all of the necessities for a household as well as an overseas stipend. I no longer had to keep my room inspection ready in the barracks and sometimes we did not have to come in to work as early if we lived off base. Life was good until it came time for me to go out on maneuvers again.

The first time I reported for maneuvers since I married was hard for me. My wife, like most German ladies I knew enjoyed getting together with their girlfriends on the weekend. They go to nightclubs to drink and enjoy music. I was a little nervous about her going out without me. Remembering my single days while hanging out in clubs, I know how some single guys think. I have seen some American soldiers getting aggressive in their pursuit of German ladies in the clubs. This was the first time I ever asked her not to go to the club without me and she agreed not to go.

This mission was a two-week maneuver exercise in a town called Munster. We went through our regular routine of training on how to set up for each area we occupied in preparation for firing rounds down range. The first week of training came to an end and on Friday we would go into the nearby town to shower and call home since we had been living and camping in the woods. We showered and rushed to get in line at the telephone booths to make our calls home. It had gotten cold, and I waited in line for an hour. I finally got to make my call home and when I called it rang several times with no answer. I hung up and called a second time and still received no answer. I hung up and walked out the booth angry. Guys will be guys and they started making jokes about what my wife was probably doing. I got a little upset, but I really could not get angry because I used to do the same thing joking to married soldiers before I got married and I now know how they felt when I heckled them. That Friday I was fuming wondering what Anke was doing. Deep down I knew she was probably in the club with her best friend Monika having a couple of drinks. I wasn't concerned about her getting drunk and making bad decisions because she never drank too much.

On Saturday I found a crew that was making a telephone run and I got on the back of their truck, all I could think about was what I was going to say to Anke if she answered the phone. We got in line and I waited thirty minutes to make a call. This time she answered, and I asked her where she was the previous night while I waited in the cold for an hour to call her. She could hear in my voice that I was angry and she told me she went to the club with Monika because Monika did not want to go by herself. She said she was sorry and would never go to the club again without me. She explained nothing happened they just had some drinks and I felt a little better. I really had no reason to distrust her. We finally came to the end of the week and a successful field exercise.

Privates were often picked for details and with my luck I was chosen to go to the railhead to guard the vehicles all night, taking shifts with other privates while everyone else was resting and preparing for the trip back home. I didn't really mind that much because I knew I would soon be home with my love. We had a particular window of time to load the vehicles because when the Germans were ready to move, we had to be ready. This task had to be completed by seven a.m. because this was the time the trains moved. It normally took about three hours but we were so excited and anxious to get home it did not take nearly that long, we finished ahead of time. I was supposed to drive my section vehicle with Sergeant Hardy even though I had pulled guard duty the night before but he was a good supervisor so he drove our vehicle. The convoy took three hours while the train took six. We arrived three hours earlier than the train but we could not get released until everyone arrived back to the base.

Arriving at the base, we had to wash all of our vehicles and park them in the motorpool in their designated places. We also had to inventory and wipe down all of our equipment before we turned it. It was the job of the armor to inspect and accept the equipment and weapons. The Armor, Specialist Reginald Riley often rejected my weapons and I had to clean it several times until they passed inspection. We got into so many arguments about cleaning my weapon and surprisingly became friends and he later became one of my best friends. Even though Riley and I became friends he still would not accept my weapon until he had rejected them at least twice, he took his job seriously and I respected him for that – though not at those moments. That was better than when he rejected it four or five times. Once all the equipment was inventoried and inspected then First Sergeant Jefferson would call a formation in which everyone had to be present. He gave us the needed information and sometimes would allow us to come in at 10 am on Monday to give us a little more time with our spouses and loved ones. He basically was giving us the weekend that they had taken from us, no one seems to care, we were just glad to get home to our spouses and girlfriends.

Anke and I spent as much time as possible alone. For the first time we didn't mind not going out to the clubs. We just wanted to stay at home and enjoy the married life. Some of her friends would come over and it seemed as if they didn't want to leave. I often had to show some kind of displeasure in order for them to get the hint that they needed to leave. We cooked dinner for her father and mother on several occasions and for Uwe, my wife's brother and his girlfriend. We also double dated with her oldest brother Manfred and his wife Birgit. It seems as if the whole family had accepted and welcomed me to the family. We knew eventually we would have to leave Germany at some point when I got reassigned to a unit in U.S.

CHAPTER 5

It was now nearing the end of my three and a half-year tour and the end of my enlistment. I really did not like the Army, and it was mainly Sergeants and Officers criticizing and being negative that affected me the most. I thought this was the norm in the Army and other units would be similar to this one. I was thankful to some of the older soldiers who knew better, and they informed me so. These soldiers had been assigned to several different units and said our current assignment was the worst that some of them had ever seen. They informed me that all army units do not spend as much time away from their families as our current unit did and convinced me to reenlist and go stateside to see how I like serving in a unit in the states. At the end of my enlistment with the love of my life standing beside me, I took the oath of enlistment for three more years. I always wanted to go to Virginia but there were not any open positions there for me. So I had to pick between Fort Carlson in Colorado, Fort Campbell in Kentucky, or Fort Lewis in Seattle. I chose Fort Lewis because neither my wife nor I knew anything about either of them so I took advice from several soldiers who had previously been stationed at these bases. After telling my wife we would be going to Fort Lewis, I went to see the retention sergeant who had insisted that I make a decision by this day so I gave him my answer and he said okay, and he would lock my assignment in for Fort Lewis. I returned to work and about an hour later I was told that the he needed me to come back to his office and when I got there I was told when he went in to lock in my assignment for Fort Lewis, an assignment popped up in Fort Eustis in Newport News, Virginia and he wanted to know if wanted to go to there instead. I quickly answered, "Yes please lock this assignment in before someone else gets it." We started making plans to relocate, excited about our new duty station

Once we received the orders it was official. We had to send our furniture ahead so it will be there by the time we got there. With a few days remaining we shipped our car, a 1988 Nissan Sentra. I rented a Mercedes to drive around while I was still out-processing. We finished these tasks, made sure our apartment was clean and ready for inspection. I turned the Mercedes back in, and we spent our last night at her parent's house because they were driving us to the airport the next morning to catch our flight in Bremen with a stopover in Frankfurt, one of the largest airports in Germany.

We were up bright and early for our flight and the time came to say our goodbyes. Anke and her mother cried so much during the two hour wait at the airport that it made me sad thinking of her leaving her family. Anke was the first in the family to move far away. Landing in Frankfurt we had a two- hour layover before our nine hour flight to New York. Our first time being in the New York airport was a culture shock, it was huge! We had to walk and go through a gate then take trains to different parts of the airport. We finally departed and two hours later we arrived in Virginia where we were met by two soldiers, The Sergeant on Duty and his driver who were waiting to take us to Fort Eustis.

Unfortunately, all of our luggage got lost. It was late Friday when we arrived. We were taken to the military hotel on base for the weekend. About three on Saturday morning the hotel staff knocked on our door stating they had put us in the wrong room. We dressed and waited in a break area until they finally found us a room. The driver picked us up Saturday morning to show us around the base and took us to look at apartments near the base. Saturday afternoon we were back at the hotel and one our suitcases finally arrived. Two of our suitcases were still missing. I had one uniform and we each had a change of clothing.

CHAPTER 6

Our two-week vacation finally came to an end. We tried to get everything in place before I reported to my new job. We had found and moved into a townhouse apartment just outside of the gate. On the first day of work our two missing damaged suitcases finally arrived just before I left our apartment. My car had not arrived yet so I got ride with a soldier who lived in my apartment complex.

I spent the day meeting the soldiers I would be working with for the next few years. There was a total of six soldiers and my section sergeant who I would be working with in the communication section. This was a different type of job from the one I did in Germany as I would be installing radios in trucks to assist the troops.

We discovered that Anke was pregnant for the second time shortly before leaving Germany. About two weeks after we arrived in Virginia Anke woke me up to tell me she thought she needed to go to the doctor because something didn't feel right. I informed my Section Sergeant Loving who told me not to come in but go to the hospital instead. Fort Eustis did not have a facility for dealing with pregnancies so we had to drive 45 minutes to Langley Air Force Base. Soon after I arrived, I got into an argument with a Lieutenant Colonel because she refused to see Anke even after I had told her that she had a miscarriage during her first trimester the previous year. This officer refused to examine her, insisting we needed to make an appointment. Another doctor overheard the discussion and said he would see her.

He agreed that the doctor was wrong in refusing treatment but let me know I could get into trouble arguing with an officer. The next morning when I got to work Anke called me crying saying she thought she has had another miscarriage. I rushed home and took her to the hospital where sadly she had in fact miscarried our child. Over the next couple months Anke had become depressed. I suspected she was under the impression that she would not be able to have kids and I began to think the same thing but I didn't want to let her know so I did my best to encourage and reassure her that everything will be fine.

Several months later we met another couple, a German wife and American husband, like us. They were living in the same complex a few apartments from where we lived and were stationed in Germany at the same time we were. James and Heike Sykes became our best friends. It turns out that Heike lived about 25 minutes from where Anke's home was and James was stationed in Bremerhaven. We all hung out in Bremerhaven but never ran into each other. Heike got Anke a job on Fort Eustis cleaning up guest rooms at the temporary lodging facility.

CHAPTER 7

ANKE BECOMES PREGNANT

Everything was going great. Anke was no longer sad and tearful. Almost every day we were either at their apartment playing cards or they were at ours. One night we were all playing cards at the Sykes' apartment when Anke felt sick. Heike starting joking that Anke might be pregnant. We were hoping she was but at the same time fearful. I was afraid if she had another miscarriage she wouldn't handle it well and I believe she thought the same thing. A few days later she got a pregnancy test, and it was positive but we didn't tell anyone until it was confirmed by a doctor. We went to Langley again and this time I remembered what I was told by the doctor that had seen her before about arguing with the officer. The pregnancy test that they did at Langley confirmed that she was indeed pregnant. We were happy and we didn't tell anyone for a while. It has often been said that good news always comes with some bad news. This statement is true in our case. The doctor noticed that she had had two miscarriages before so he told her that she had to take a leave of absence from work. This pregnancy is considered high risk because of her previous miscarriages and to be cautious he wanted her to stay home until she gave birth. We didn't like it but we knew it was what was best if we wanted to become proud parents.

For the duration of her pregnancy Anke was confined to bedrest. My life became miserable. Coming home from work daily dealing with her sitting at home imagining that I am looking at other women, or when I came home, she wanted to go walking and swimming became draining. All I wanted to do was rest after work but I knew if I didn't support her and participate in activities she chose, she would get angry and start wrongly accusing me so I gave in.

Working with this group of soldiers was much different than the crews in Germany. Everyone seemed to work on their own. Right away one of the guys I connected with was Specialist Christopher Scott. He was the section clown. He was constantly making jokes, doing things to make everyone laugh, and getting into trouble with the Sergeant in Charge. When this sergeant tried to correct him, he only became worse, making others laugh in this process. He became one of my best friends. We both enjoyed sports and spent a lot time together in the gyms on the base and wherever there was a game we were there,

It was August 1990 and Anke was due in October. On August 2 Saddam Hussein's forces invaded Kuwait and the next day we were called in to bring our gear for possible deployment. We thought we were just being called in as routine evaluation to check our readiness. Much to our surprise this was not the case. We were ordered to remain on base and the gates were locked. We were told that we were deploying as result of this invasion and to give the soldiers that worked in the orderly room our telephone numbers. These clerks were supposed to contact our spouses and tell them we were not coming back home and were deploying. I decided that it would not be a good ideal for my wife to hear this from someone else so I made up an excuse saying I need to go back home because I left some of the items I needed to be ready to deploy. They believed me, let me go, and told me to hurry back. I got home and just as I had expected she did not handle this news well. I was even more afraid because she was seven months pregnant. I contacted James and Heike and I dropped Anke off at their apartment. After two weeks of being locked on the base our families were allowed to come on the base to see us. After a month of being restricted to the base we were finally released. Our battalion was broken down into detachments. I thought I was lucky because my detachment didn't deploy. Then I got orders to go to a military leadership school in Fort Knox, Kentucky. I immediately planned to turn it down and go on a later date because I wanted to be there when my son was born but my section chief at this time, Sergeant First Class Larry Philips informed me the best thing I can do for my family is go to this school as planned. This would increase my chances of getting promoted to Sergeant so I could make more money for the family. It was believed that once you turned down a military school the Sergeant Major would make sure you never got another chance to go to the school.

In September 1990, I flew from Norfolk to Fort Knox to begin Primary Leadership Development Course (PLDC). I was unhappy because I would not be present with my wife when our son was born. Several weeks into the course, every night we talked. A few days before he was born, I started stressing because I could not contact my wife at our home. On October 20th, my roommate at school who was also stationed at Fort Eustis, was talking to his wife, and told me that she had given birth to their child. I asked him to see if she knew how I could find out about my wife. She told him that another lady had given birth the same day as she did and they were in the same room. I asked his wife to find out the lady's name. It turns out that it was Anke. I thought it was an odd coincidence that I was roommates with her husband in Kentucky and she was roommates with my wife at Langley in the base hospital. I was relieved and happy knowing that my wife had given birth to our son and both of them were fine. Much to my surprise she named him Kenneth Jr. We had discussed what we would name him, we didn't think about too many names. We just wanted her to get birth to a healthy baby.

CHAPTER 8

MEETING MY SON FOR THE FIRST TIME

Late November when I arrived at Norfolk Airport my wife and our son Kenneth Jr were waiting for me and I was able to see him before we headed back to Fort Eustis. After spending a week with my family, I was once again alerted early that Saturday morning to report back to the base. We went through a couple of hours of training and then told to go back home and informed it was a good chance that we would deploy in December. The second week of December we were alerted again and given information and instructions about what to expect once we deployed. We were told our time to deploy would be soon and we were released. When I arrived home, my wife was crying because they had called and told her I had to come back to the base as soon as possible because I was deploying from Langley that same day. I tried to calm her down and called our closest friends James and Heike because I did not want her to be alone with our child. They agreed to let her stay with them a few days. I went back to Fort Eustis and was informed that I would be deployed to Desert Storm.

I arrived at Langley with a captain and another driver. Once we got checked in, I called my wife to meet me at Langley for lunch. She and Kenny Jr. arrived and we had lunch I as I attempted to calm her down. I explained to her that we would stay there for a couple of days and then we will return to Fort Eustis. This had happened on several occasions. After lunch she dropped me back off to where she had picked me up and we said our goodbyes. The Master Sergeant that was in charge of putting units on the manifest to fly out of Langley got upset with one unit and decided to bump them off of the manifest and put us on the flight. I deployed with the Captain and another E-4 and our vehicles. We arrived and rested for about two hours as the plane was refueled. Two hours later we landed in Saudi Arabi and were there about three days before the rest of our unit joined us. We supported 12 units that consisted of Reserves and National Guard units. We were there for Desert Storm and Desert Shield. The war ended in February 1991. We finally received orders to return home in May of 1991.

We arrived back at Fort Eustis late at night. We were all excited to finally be back and seeing our love ones after being gone five months felt amazing. We had to be debriefed and our inventory accounted for and turned in before we were released to join our families. There were celebrations accompanied by speeches by senior ranking officers as well as city officials from the Newport News area.

The next several days we were also welcomed back by the city giving those who served in the Gulf War discounts on meals at certain restaurants as well as theme parks. I think most of us were just glad to be back with our loved ones. We were also given free leave which enabled us to spend more time with families there and in other places.

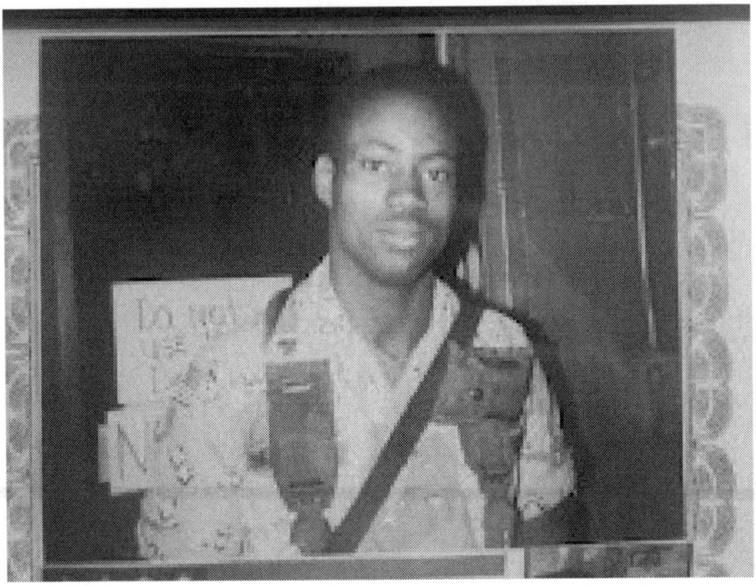

CHAPTER 9

THE DECISION

Being alerted and eventually deploying to the Gulf War really put everything in perspective. We realized that in a moment's notice our lives could be changed forever as we all witnessed with the Gulf War. I had been weighing my options even before the war. During the war I had come to the conclusion that I would leave the Army once I returned to Fort Eustis.

Our first day at work was a continuation of what we had started before we shipped our equipment home. Eventually the time would come when I had to make the decision whether to leave the Army or continue serving. Certainly, I had to talk it over with my wife because it would be a life changing event for her as well. Anke was fearful of me leaving the military because it was a good life with the exception of the deployment to the Gulf War.

The decision was made that we would stay in the Army only if we could go back to Germany. I set that plan into motion when I reported to the Retention Sergeant and told her my intentions. She went to work trying to find me a position in Germany. I think she became concerned that she would be unable to find me a position. She called me several times asking if she could not find me a position would I still reenlist? I responded to her request each time with an answer of "No!"

In August 1991 my family and I took thirty days leave to go back to visit her family in Germany. Before we departed for our vacation, I contacted the retention Sergeant to let her know that I would be in Germany for thirty days. I gave her my in-laws telephone number and told her to call me as soon as she found me a position in Germany and I would return and reenlist. About ten days into our vacation I received a call from the her confirming that she had found my desired position and asked when I would be back to reenlist. The whole family was excited that we would be coming back to Germany after living for two years in Virginia.

We arrived back to Fort Eustis in September. As soon as I returned to work I reported to the Retention Sergeant to get the paperwork started. Within three days we had all the paperwork completed. My wife and my one year old son were present as I took the oath of enlistment for a three year term. The paperwork was done and we thought we would be back in Germany for the Christmas holidays. I got my orders and to our dismay, our arrival in Germany would be February 1992. My wife and her family were sad because we were all looking forward to spending Christmas together. I had to do something to fix this problem and spent several days thinking of how to rectify the situation. By this time our best friends James and Heike had gotten their orders to go return to Germany and we were sad that we would be separating. James told me to check with the section that did our orders to see if they were aware that my wife was German. I thought they knew this however I brought it to their attention that my wife was German and she could stay with her parents until housing was available at our new duty station. I went to the section that was responsible for cutting orders for duty assignments and began talking with one of the clerks who reviewed my orders. He told me that I could not leave early because they had to find housing for my family before we could go to Germany. I informed him that rule did not apply to me and my family and I explained that my wife was German and she and my son could live with her family in Germany until they could find housing for us. He talked to his supervisor and came back and told me if I could get a letter from her parents stating that they could stay with them they would see what they could do about changing my reporting date. In about four days we had the letter in hand and I could hardly wait to take it to the orders section. When I delivered the letter to the clerk he told me to come back in about a day. I came back the next day and received my new orders. My reporting day changed from February 1992 to November 1991. With my new orders in hand, I told my wife and she told her family. We were all filled with joy knowing that we would spending Christmas together and living in Germany once again.

CHAPTER 10

ARRIVING BACK IN GERMANY

We arrived November 1991 to Frankfurt International Airport. There were vans at the airport to transport service members and their families to the 21st Replacement Center in Frankfurt. This is where soldiers and family members are processed into the country. It was here that I found out that the unit I was being assigned to was returning from Desert Storm. I was assigned to 11th Army Cavalry Regiment stationed at Bad Kissingen Germany. The Headquarters were in Fulda. After spending a night in a hotel, we were transported from Frankfurt by van to Fulda. Arriving in Fulda we had to also be processed into 11th ACR headquarters. There my family and I were picked up by a young soldier named PFC Marvin Hill. PFC HILL was in the same section in which I would be assigned.

During this three-year tour 11th ACR moved from Bad Kissingen to Wildflecken. During this tour I was also separated from my family once again for four months. I was selected to go to a Military Leadership School called Basic Noncommission Officer Course (BNOC). I had sworn to myself that I would never leave my family for such a long period as I had already done when I was deployed to the Gulf War for five months. My wife convinced me to go to this school because she did not want my military career to end. A few months later I departed Germany heading to Augusta,

Georgia to this school leaving my wife and two-year-old son. This would turn out to be a very difficult time for us.

I finally completed this school and graduated which ensured that my career would continue. My wife and son met me in Frankfurt. Upon arriving back to my unit in Wildflecken I was informed that 11th ACR was deactivating. I was glad to be home with my family but I didn't realize that I would not be able to talk to my son. The four months that I was in school in Augusta, Anke only spoke German to him. I returned home and could not talk to him because he no longer understood English and I didn't understand German. It was a few weeks before he could understand me.

My first day back to work I received some bad news. I was pulled off the duty I had been assigned to, told to report to my First Sergeant's office, and I was informed that The American Red Cross had called and told him that my mom had passed away. The Red Cross arraigned everything within a few hours and my family was on a plane heading back to Georgia. My mother's death was hard for me because she was always the one that kept me focused and motivated to accomplish whatever goal that was before me. After her funeral a few days later, we were on a plane heading back to Germany. As result of my unit deactivating, I had been reassigned with my family to Babenhausen, Germany. They were in full deactivating mode when we arrived back in Wildflecken. I started out processing as soon as arrived back on the post.

I arrived to Babenhausen with my family and was assigned to the 25th field Artillery unit. I would finish my last eighteen months of my tour with A battery 2ND AND 5th field Artillery. I was planning on trying to extend my tour in Germany. The Department of the Army however had others plans for me and I had already received an assignment to report to Fort Hood in Killeen, Texas.

CHAPTER 11

ARRIVING AT FORT HOOD

My family and I arrived at Fort Hood Army Base November 1994. I was assigned to 4th Battalion 5th Air Defense Artillery. I was assigned to D company. My son Kenny Jr. was now four years old. We bought a house in Killeen, about fifteen minutes from the base. It was here where Kenny Jr. started to develop into an athlete.

I didn't have any close friends while stationed at Fort Hood until a young soldier arrived at the unit that I was assigned to. His name was Sergeant Raymond Crandell. I saw his patch of the unit that he was coming from and realized he was stationed in Garlstedt just as I had been. One day we started talking about Garlstedt, I left in 1989 and he arrived in 1990. We knew and went to some of the same places. We had several things in common and one of them was we both played basketball. We became close friends and our families became friends. He had a daughter who played well with our son. We even got in trouble a couple times with the wives because we were spending too much time in the gym.

Kenny was five years old when started to dunk on a five foot basketball goal. I thought to myself "This kid may emerge to be a good basketball player." I signed him up to play on his first basketball team. He was not a scorer on this team but he rebounded the ball well. He also played soccer that year and emerged as one the best soccer players for his age group. I guess it was natural for him to play soccer well because he is half German and they are known for being good soccer players. His mother thought he was going to be a soccer player but I had other plans for him that I kept to myself.

In 1996 the Department of the Army selected me to become an Army Recruiter. This was not in my plans. I tried to get the orders changed but was unsuccessful. By this time, I had been working with Kenny to develop his skills in basketball, baseball, and soccer. In January 1997 I started my training to become an Army Recruiter at the Army Recruiting School at Fort Jackson Army Base in Columbia, South Carolina. After the completion of this six-week school I returned back to Fort Hood. The Great Lakes Recruiting command had assigned me to a recruiting station in Muskegon, Michigan. Our headquarters was located in Lansing.

CHAPTER 12

ARRIVING IN MUSKEGON MICHIGAN

In May 1997 my family and I departed from Fort Hood heading to Muskegon where I would start my career as an Army Recruiter. Our first weekend in Muskegon we were snowed in. This is in the middle of May and there was snow on the ground. After a few weeks of being in Muskegon we found an apartment in North Muskegon. Kenny and I continued his training in basketball, baseball and soccer. Anke and I went to a doctor's office to get a diagnosis of the possible lump she had found in her breast. A few days later it was confirmed that Anke had breast cancer. We were assured that it was treatable and she would be fine. The doctors said they caught it early and since she was so young her treatment did not have to be so aggressive so they decided to try chemo first and radiation later.

Anke started the treatments. The first few treatments of chemo were not that bad. After several treatments she started to get weaker and sicker and could no longer eat. Her parents came to visit to help us for about a month. She was frequently hospitalized because her blood count would drop too low. She still encouraged me to continue training with Kenny. He played in a soccer league and did well, being one of the best soccer players in his age group once again. Anke attended some of the soccer games when she was able. Kenny played so well that he became known to all the parents and we instantly had friends because of him. At an early age it seems that he had the ability to bring people together with his outstanding athletic ability.

In September of that year, we had to move to another apartment, Anke was unable to go up and down stairs anymore. Luckily, we found some new apartments that were being built not far from where we were currently living. We were able to locate the people that were renting the apartments and I explained to them our situation so they agreed to let us rent one of the apartments. This was great because Anke didn't have to be bothered with stairs anymore and could venture outside, no longer being stuck indoors.

A few days before the move we didn't know how we were going to get everything moved into our new apartment. The day of the move we were amazed as some of Anke's nurses and their husbands, some of Kenny's teammates' parents, and some my recruiters helped us move into our new apartment. We were amazed at the love that was shown to my family during these difficult times.

CHAPTER 13

ENCOUNTERING THE FIRST TRAGEDY

Anke spent six months in and out of the hospital. At times we didn't see Kenny much because he was spending a lot of time at the homes of his friends while we were back and forth with treatment. Anke's parents had gone back to Germany. A week later they came back because her health had worsened. November 5, 1997, Anke my wife of 10 years and Kenny's mother passed away, sixteen days after he had celebrated his 7th birthday.

We took Anke home to be buried in Germany. After the funeral we spent about week with her parents and were back on a plane heading back to Muskegon, about to begin life full of uncertainty. I am sure that he was just as scared as I was not knowing where we would go from here. I began trying to fill the role of father and mother which was exhausting at times. I became doubtful about my ability to be a single parent and didn't want him to miss out on anything. Just looking at him knowing that he was depending on me to get him through these difficult times was a bit overwhelming. I truly believe it was his motivation that got me up in the morning and kept me going. The times when I became depressed, I kept pushing through because I knew I had to be strong for him. Much to our surprise, when we arrived back to Muskegon we received an abundance of assistance. We didn't have to ask but Kenny's teammates' parents had gotten together and worked out a schedule in which they would pick Kenny up from school. They even helped him with his homework and I would pick him up from their homes and take him to our home.

After about two months things had started to become frustrating with some of the parents because I was still an Army recruiter and I worked long hours. I knew that this would eventually become a problem. I had already begun talking to my command about possible solutions. In the meantime, Kenny continued with his training through these difficult times. Every Saturday we would spend several hours at the boys and girls club. He would spend a couple of hours in the pool and I would be in the water with him doing drills. After showering we worked on basketball drills for another two hours before heading home. He would spend several hours a day when I got off early and on the weekend shooting on his goal outside. Years later he told a reporter from a newspaper that those hours he spent shooting outside by himself were spent memorizing everything he could about his mother. He said that he wanted to ensure that he would not forget anything about her.

The Great Lakes Army Recruiting command asked me if I wanted to return to the regular Army now since I was now a single parent. I informed them if they let me go to my hometown Warner Robins, Georgia to recruit I would continue my three-year commitment as a part of the Army Recruiting Command. They granted my request and put me on assignment to the Atlanta Army Recruiting Command.

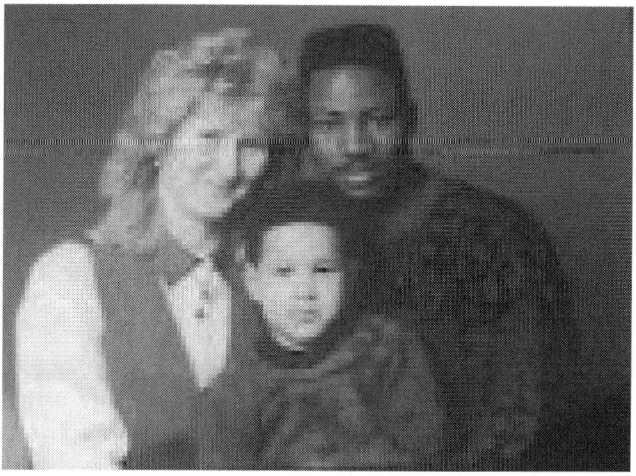

CHAPTER 14

ARRIVING IN WARNER ROBINS GEORGIA

In March 1998 we arrived in Warner Robins. It was exciting finally being able to live in my hometown and spend time with my family and old friends. We bought a home in neighboring Bonaire. I hired a live-in nanny, a young lady I had gotten to know in Michigan that had worked in the Recruiting office there.

We enrolled Kenny in school and right away we began his training once again. Now he was playing soccer and baseball. He did well in both sports. He made the All-Star team in both sports both seasons he played in Warner Robins.

Several months passed and I meet a young lady in church. Her name was Tracy Stewart. Tracy was a joyous person. She had two sisters who had passed away when they were young and she was the surviving child of Cal and Ann Stewart. Creative, funny, strong-willed, beautiful, and loving, this was a woman who loved God, her family, church, and everybody she met. She wrote beautiful poetry, doted on her family, was a great cook, and was well loved in our church and community.

We dated for a few months. She got along well with Kenny Jr. and things seem to be getting back normal for Kenny and me. I had noticed on several occasions there were activities at the school where other kids would be there with both parents and it would just be Kenny and me. It seems as though he was missing that mother figure in his life. I did everything I could to make him feel as if he was like the other kids in his class and my relationship with Tracy began to progress to the point where I thought that she would be a wonderful wife and a good mother figure for Kenny. I talked to Kenny before I talked to Tracy to see what he thought about it. I wanted him to know if things worked out, she would become a part of our family and live in our home with us. I also made sure he knew that Tracy was not trying to replace his mother, she loved him as well and would be there for us. After several weeks of discussing the situation with him, I asked if he thought we should get married and he said yes. Kenny and I picked the ring together. He was there when I proposed to Tracy and she said yes. We begin planning our wedding together.

The day finally came. September 13, 1998 Tracy and I were married. Once again, I had a wife and Kenny had a stepmother. Kenny was no longer an only child, he had a brother. Even though he was already grown Kenny was glad to have a big brother. Nathaniel (Nate) Stewart was also added to our family with his wife Tamika and son Brandon. I became a husband, a father for the second time, a father in-law, and a grandfather all the same day. The honeymoon was great we spent a week in Cancun Mexico and returned home to begin our adventure together.

I had to do a lot a paperwork to get Tracy processed into the military life and government system. This would enable her to get a military identification card and all the benefits of being married to a soldier. It did take a few months for us to get used to living together. Kenny liked having Tracy around all the time however, like all kids, he had to see what he could get away with. Sometimes he tested her and acted out. When he saw that she was not going to let him get away with misbehaving, he gave up and accepted her as part of the family. Tamika was pregnant with twins and gave birth to Jeremy and Brian in December that year. My family again grew and we loved being included in such a wonderful unit.

Along with soccer and baseball Kenny also played football but this didn't last long. Although he was pretty good and learned the game quickly because I was training him but he lost interest and dedicated himself more to soccer and baseball. I had played several years of football as a child and was pretty good. As luck would have it the coach got selected for jury duty. The coach asked me to take over for him because I was at practice the majority of the time. I was supposed to be out recruiting but I would cut my hours short so I could be at his practices. We all were adjusting well as a new family. His season came to end.

In 1998 I had to make a decision if I was going to reenlist and remain in the Army on active duty. I was considering getting out and opening a day care center, a dream Tracy and I had, but this was not progressing fast enough and I had to make a decision quickly on my enlistment. I made the decision to reenlist and this enlistment would take me to the retirement date in 2006.

Sergeant Loving and I were counting the days to when we would both be leaving the recruiting command and returning back to our regular jobs in the Army. We were thirty days out from leaving the recruiting status behind us when one day our Station Commander called us into his office. He told us he had some good news and some bad news. The good news was one of us would get to leave recruiting status early and the other would be extended for two months. With my luck I was the one that got extended for two month and Sergeant Loving got a chance to leave recruiting a month early.

I got a chance to pick where I would be stationed once I departed from the recruiting command. Tracy wanted to stayed close to home so she could be near her parents so we chose to go to Fort Stewart in Hinesville, Georgia. I had heard that this was not a good duty assignment but I wanted Tracy to be happy. Nate and his family lived in Jacksonville Florida, about two hours away. The time came and I out processed from Atlanta Battalion Recruiting Command July 2000. We all were exciting about our new assignment.

CHAPTER 15

ARRIVING AT FORT STEWART

We arrived at Fort Stewart and moved into our new home in Hinesville. Our new house was about twenty minutes from the back gate of the base. I took about thirty days of vacation and we spent that time getting Kenny registered at his new school. Tracy had told me once we started dating that she had been diagnosis with Sarcoidosis years ago. This was a lung disease and she assured me that she was fine and I didn't have anything to be worried about. She had some trying times including an aneurysm years before but was told by her doctors this was not discerning. After losing Anke, I always found a way to ask about medical conditions before I started a relationship. Some of the women I met were turned off by my questions. While I didn't want to seem rude or invasive, I had to do whatever was necessary to try to protect us from experiencing such tragedy again. Tracy didn't have any problems with me asking questions. I was told also that because of Tracy's health, I could put her on the exceptional family member program.

A few days before I was scheduled to report into my new Battalion, I went to the Brigade Sergeant Major's office to talk about the exceptional family member program. The Sergeant Major I needed to talk to was away and my Battalion Sergeant Major was filling in for him. He told me that his wife did not need to go on the program because his wife and daughter had the same disease and they were fine.

When my leave was up, I reported to work, eager to start my job as a supervisor for several soldiers. Tracy had started having some health problems. She started seeing a doctor in Savannah because her hometown of Macon and her specialist of many years was over two hours away. At her first appointment with the new doctor, he examined her records and told her she should have never been on steroids for that long period of time. His plan was to wean her off and reduce the dosage of steroids with the hope that they had not caused any damage to her body. Tracy was in agreement because the steroids were causing her to gain weight. The doctor started reduce her dosage of steroids. One day she started having difficulty catching her breath. She went to the doctor and they put her on oxygen but after several hours she was better. She started having problems breathing regularly and her doctor put her on medication so that she had to take breathing treatments several times a day. Tracy decided that it would probably be easier if she just took small oxygen tanks with her every time she went somewhere. Things were hectic at times because we always had to make sure that we had several tanks always on hand. Sometimes we would either run out of oxygen with the tanks that we had or we didn't bring enough and had to locate a place where we could get more tanks.

It came time for me to go out and do maneuvers with my new unit. I was somewhat nervous about leaving her but by this time she was very much dependent upon these oxygen tanks. I had to go because it was a part of the job I had been assigned to. We mostly stayed in contact while I was out doing maneuvers. We made it through one week of training.

We celebrated Kenny's birthday on October 20th. A few days later she had gotten much weaker. She was hardly getting out of the bed. She was only able at times to get up and go to the bathroom. I find myself doing everything with the hope of her resting and getting better. By this time Kenny was now 10 years old and he helped out a lot.

CHAPTER 16

TRAGEDY STRIKES AGAIN

On the first day of November in 2000, I was at work and Kenny was at school. Tracy called to tell me she thought she was having a heart attack. I called 911 and when I arrived home she was in the ambulance. She told me to get Kenny situated after school and then come to the hospital. We really didn't know anyone well because we had just moved to Hinesville. There was a couple that lived across the street from us we had spoken several times. I went over to their house and explained Tracy was in the hospital and asked if Kenny could spend the night with them. I also asked if they could put him on the bus for school the next day and assuring them that I would be back home by the time he gets out of school. When I arrived at the hospital she had slipped into a coma. The next day her parents, Cal and Ann, Nate and Tamika, and their three kids arrived. The doctors said that the first 24 hours were critical and although she was in a coma the doctors were optimistic that she would recover. We all took turns spending time with her, praying for a positive outcome.

Tracy's birthday was November 7th but we didn't get to celebrate her birthday because her condition had not improved. On Veteran's Day, November 11th, many of her relatives visited. All them took turns going in to spend time with her. Her family members started departing for home in the afternoon and I was going back and forth with her family members as they took turns visiting in her Intensive Care Unit room as others were in the waiting room. Tracy's mother, other relatives, and I were getting ready to leave and Tracy's dad had already headed home. I decided to go and check on Tracy and as I turned the corner, I looked into Tracy's room and saw several doctors there. I knew this was not a good sign but not knowing what it meant, I went and spoke to her mom and relatives and we went into a smaller waiting room. A few minutes later a doctor came and told us Tracy had passed away. Her mom was in shock, so I called her father and told him that she was gone. Cal came back to the hospital to be with us. I called Nate and told him he needed to come back to the hospital, not divulging the seriousness because he was driving. When he arrived Ann and I told him the bad news. Kenny by this time understood the gravity of the circumstances and dealing with death because he had experienced it before but his nephews were too young to understand what was happening.

    Once again Kenny and I had suffered the loss of a wife and parent. Not knowing what was next in our lives I tried to be strong for him after losing his mother and now his stepmom. Everyone gathered at Tracy's parents' house as they arranged everything for the funeral. I didn't care about any attention. I sat alone on a sofa in her parent's house while everyone was checking on them and other family members. The Stewart family had been through so much with the death of now all of the Stewart daughters. Cal, Ann, Nate and his family were devastated but their faith helped them endure other storms and together as a family, they will also weather this one. This was a large and close family. Generations would gather for holidays and everyday events. The family home was full of love, laughter, and an abundance of delicious Southern cooking. Family and friends flocked around Ann, concerned for her health. Many knew she had been struggling for some time with her health but always putting others before herself.

Tracy and I had only been married a little over two years but in that short time, our lives were greatly enriched with the presence of her and her family. As time passed, Kenny and I spent a lot of time with her parents on weekends and holidays. Kenny became very close with his grandparents, Nate and his family. Kenny was glad to have a big brother, a sister-in-law, nephews, and such a great support group.

When the family gathered at the Stewart's home prior to her funeral, I sat quietly alone. The house was crowded as arrangements were being made for Tracy's funeral. Many of her friends weren't well acquainted with me as we hadn't lived in her hometown long after we married. One of their church members and friends, Elnora noticed I was sitting alone and came over to talk to me.

My birthday was December 4th and evidently Tracy's mother told Elnora it was coming up. Elnora called Tracy's parent's home and I answered the phone. She explained who she was and I remembered her. She asked me what was I doing for my birthday and I had no plans so Elnora invited me out to dinner. I asked Ann what she thought and Ann convinced me to let her take me out for my birthday.

CHAPTER 17

TRAGEDY STRIKES AGAIN

Ann had been sick for much of her life. She had three beautiful daughters and Tracy was her last child to succumb to death. Ann had been a caregiver and as is often the case, she was busy caring for others, often neglecting her health. In spite of her poor health, she put on a brave face and had to admit that she was ill while trying desperately to return to her normal activities. Nate, Tamika, and their three rambunctious sons were accustomed to depending on Tracy so Ann attempted to step in. The boys were quite a handful, Brandon was the oldest at five, and two year old twins Jeremy and Brian full of energy, curiosity, and joy. The Stewart family was large and very close and the death of Tracy filled a void that was evident.

In January I received a call from Ann's niece, Patricia informing me Ann went to a doctor's appointment and because she was experiencing difficulty breathing, they admitted her to the hospital. That weekend Kenny and I went to Macon to spend time with the family. The next week Patricia told me Ann would have to have open heart surgery, I was not able to be there for the surgery but Patricia and I had become close and she kept me abreast on the status of her condition, informing me later that the surgery went well and Ann was recovering nicely. That weekend Kenny and I were heading back to Macon to visit the family.

In February Kenny and I had been to Macon for the weekend and were getting ready to head back to Fort Stewart. We stopped by the hospital to see Ann on our way out. I walked into her room and several members of the church were there and Ann was entertaining them all. That is who she was, she loved entertaining people. I was upset because the doctor's instructions to us that she was not supposed to have too many visitors at one time. Somehow, the nurse had not noticed or she didn't care about all the people that were in her room. I told them that they had to leave and explained that according to the doctor's orders she could only have two visitors at a time and I believe it was about seven people in her room. The nurse walked in and said Ann needed her sleep, echoing my warning that Ann needed to rest. Almost everyone left and we spent a few minutes with her and said our goodbyes. Macon was approximately 2 hours from Fort Stewart. An hour into our drive I got a call from Patricia telling me that she had taken a turn for the worst. Monday at work I got a called from Patricia and she told me that she was not going to get any better, they were waiting for her to pass away. Several hours later Patricia called me and told me that Anne was gone. Once again, Kenny and I were dealing with a loss of another close family member.

Days had passed and Kenny and I started trying to continue with our regular daily activities. It was basketball season and we thought this would be a good way to keep our minds off of dealing with the grief of losing Tracy and Ann. We continued practicing every chance we got. This was the season when I realized that he could probably be a pretty good player. He hadn't played basketball for several years.

He was over five feet tall and he was taller than most kids his age. That season he emerged as a shooter and he was unstoppable. He was rebounding, making shots and getting to the basketball. He had become a complete player. That year there only one kid that gave him any trouble and he was actually older and was not supposed to be playing in the same league as Kenny. I believe they allowed him to play in that league because his father was the coach.

That year Kenny's team did pretty well because he was such an all- around player. They made it to the second round of the playoffs but got beat by the team with the kid that was not supposed to be playing in that league. At the end of the season Kenny made the All-Star team. The older kid was a few inches taller and he and Kenny played well together on the All-Star team, they were the top two players in the league that year. Kenny averaged about 15 points per game and the older kid averaged about 18 points per game.

By this time Elnora had become a good friend and she had started spending time with us. It was kind of weird but it started to feel like we were already a family. I believe Kenny felt good about seeing her in the stands at his games. She was cheering the loudest at every game.

Baseball season began and Kenny had played well in the league in Warner Robins before moving to Hinesville. He continued to perform well and excelled in baseball too. He played first base and was also a good hitter. His team made the playoffs but was beaten in the first round. At the end of the season, once again Kenny made the All-Star team. They played well but did not advance to the second round.

Kenny and I were faced with another difficult decision, deciding whether or not I should stay on active duty. It was very trying being a single parent and overseeing 16 soldiers at work. I found myself spending more time with the soldiers than I was spending with my son. It seemed that the unit was trying to set me up to fail. All 16 soldiers were badly behaved, I did not have one good soldier in my squad. Every offense from arrests to being placed in the Psychiatric Ward. I had to go to court with several soldiers and visit soldiers in the Psych Wards. It had become a nightmare. By this time, I had completed 15 years in the Army with five more to go. I tried to change my job, tried to relocate to another base, I even considered going to another branch of service so that I would not lose the 15 years that I had served. No one was willing to help me. Since I was at a base known for rapid deployments and regular field exercises, the thought of deploying to another war zone scared me because I didn't know how Kenny would respond. I once had to go out and do maneuvers for a week. I had to ask Elnora to come and stay with Kenny for that week that I was gone. I could tell that he was scared that something would happen to me. I ensured him that everything was going to be okay. Elnora told me the first couple of days he was quiet and he acted more withdrawn than usual. Elnora was impressed that Kenny got himself up each morning when his alarm clock chimed, had breakfast, took Shiloh outside, fed him, and got on the bus without any assistance. At 10 he also washed his own clothes and was more responsible than kids she had seen much older. Coming home from school he was able to get a snack, take Shiloh outside for exercise and do his chores without having to be prompted. He was considerate, smart, and responsible. While I was in the field, she took Kenny to his practices or games and they visited Baskin Robbins every day for ice cream, a passion they shared.

A Senior Ranking NCO told me less than two months after Tracy passed away that I had been given six weeks to grieve so it was now time for me to move on. When I told them I didn't have anyone to leave Kenny with when I deployed for training, I was told to put him in 24 hour day care. That didn't exist at my base and if it did, what kind of parent would I be to leave him with relative strangers when we were both enduring such a time of uncertainty?

After trying everything possible to stay in the Army and failing miserably, I came to the decision that the best thing for us was for me to leave the military. When I told my command my decision, they thought I was crazy. They said that I was not going to throw away 15 years. I told them that I had considered that and didn't want to but it was what was best for Kenny and me. At this point, they did everything to try and keep me from leaving the military. It was not because they cared so much about me and my well-being, it was more about the fact that the Army had let too many soldiers use the early out option because in 1992 they paid soldiers to leave the military and now they were short staffed of seasoned and qualified senior soldiers. It had been decided in the early 1990's that our military was too big and nine years later they realized they let too many soldiers go. They needed to hold on to the soldiers that they had left. They got rid of the three- and four-year options. Once a soldier reached 10 years, they had to enlist for an additional 10 more years. The Army even stopped guaranteeing a 20-year retirement. Once a soldier reached 20 years, they had to submit a request to retire, and it could and sometimes did not get approved. This resulted in soldiers being forced to stay in past 20 years against their will.

Before Ann passed away, she often told me if I had trouble trying to get out the military to contact Elnora and she would probably know what do or who to talk to. No one on the base would help me file the necessary paperwork for me to get out of the Army. The Sergeant Major had threatened that if anyone helped, they would face punishment under the Uniform Code of Military Justice (UCMJ). As a result, I could get no one to help from the base personnel office. I turned to Elnora who had become a friend. I explained to her what was going on. I have gotten letters from my preachers and from doctors that all stated that I should be allowed to receive a hardship discharge. However, my command did not see it that way. Elnora had been a Union President for the post office. She contacted Senator Saxby Chambliss' representative and they explained to her what I had to do. After explaining it to me she realized I had no idea what she was talking about. One night we went to her union office and she typed the paperwork up and filled out all the necessary forms. We dropped everything off at the Senator's office the next day.

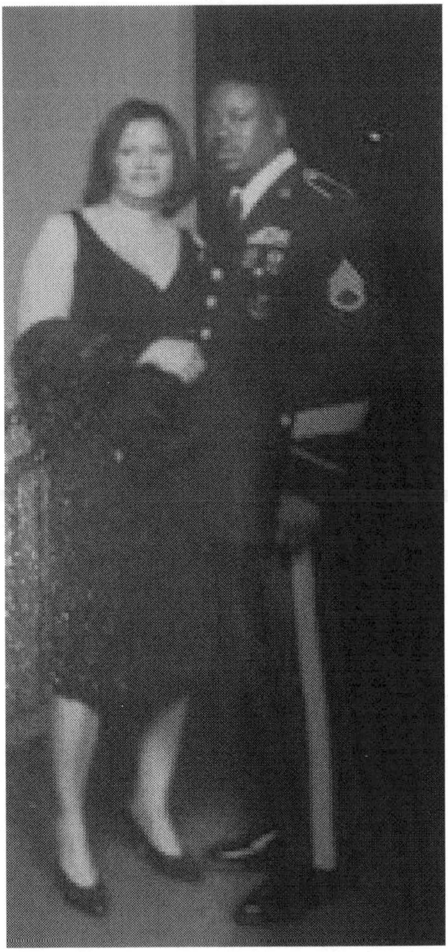

CHAPTER 18

THE FINAL ENCOUNTER WITH MY CHAIN OF COMMAND

The next Monday morning, we were doing maintenance on all our vehicles in the motor pool. I received a message that I had to go to the Battalion where all the higher-ranking NCOs and Officers have their offices. I again figured I was in trouble. I walked in the office and there were three of the higher-ranking Noncommissioned officers and three of the higher-ranking Officers waiting for me. I was the lowest ranking soldier present. It was probably the first time I had ever seen a Full Bird Colonel. I walked in the office and one of the senior ranking NCOs asked me if I got permission to do a congressional Inquiry. I didn't really know how to answer this question. I asked him if I was supposed to get permission. He responded no so I answered that is why I didn't ask for permission. All six of these high-ranking soldiers verbally attacked me and curse words were used. This Congressional is a big deal. This complaint against my chain of command shone the light on that post and its leaders. The illegal actions that were taking place on this Army base would be discovered. Now political and military leaders were watching how this base conducted its day-to-day business and treating soldiers under their care. Being under the microscope, they had to do everything by the book or they would find themselves being written up or relieved of their command. This Congressional Inquiry forced them to give me a hardship discharge. This was also an honorable discharge so if my circumstances changed, I could come back on active duty, finish my time and retire.

I was told by a Sergeant First Class that was retiring that one of senior noncommissioned officers had called a formation with the whole battalion. And everyone that was in formation was informed that no one was allowed to talk to me for the duration of my remaining enlistment at Fort Stewart. They were threatened if they were caught talking to me, they would receive punishment under UCMJ. They didn't want these soldiers to talk to me because they knew many of the soldiers on this base were not happy being there. The command was afraid that they might question me on how to get out of the Army. It was no longer a secret that I had taken on the chain command and won.

On June 30th I was cleared from the base and was doing my final out-processing. It was my decision to revisit my plan from 1985 to become a gospel preacher in the church of Christ. This had been my dream since I was 15 years old and I preached my first sermon.

CHAPTER 19

AVERTING ANOTHER ALMOST TRAGEDY

By this time Elnora Seabrooks and I had been dating for several months. I found myself in love with the young lady that told me from the beginning that she was not going anywhere. Taking in consideration what Kenny and I been through with the passing of my previous wives. I proposed after of course discussing it with Kenny Jr. and she said yes. We planned our wedding but less than two weeks before our wedding date, my father passed away of a heart attack. We had his funeral on August 4 and our wedding the next week on August 11, 2001. Elnora and I were married in my hometown of Warner Robins. Her two adult children, Calvin and Alysha were added to our family.

We honeymooned in Jamaica, moving into a rental house in Lakeland, and I started attending the Florida of School of Preaching the next week. While attending the Florida School of Preaching we were not allowed to work doing school because we took ten classes a semester thereby finishing four years of studies in two years. Everything was going well but things were a little stressful because we had to live on the support of churches and others while attending the Florida School of Preaching. The course load was also strenuous. Elnora had been able to work a couple of jobs through a temp agency and had been hired in the Human Resources office at Publix, a regional grocery store headquartered there.

In October 20th we had celebrated Kenny's 11th birthday. A few days later, I started to feel sick, complaining about being hot and thirsty but I continued attending school, driving back and forth to classes. One night it got so bad I could not sleep and I kept tossing and turning, becoming lethargic. I put a cold washcloth on my head and was sweating profusely. Elnora started asking simple questions that I couldn't answer, I didn't remember what day it was, the last day I could recall was Kenny's birthday. I remembered who Kenny was and I also remembered my dog, Shiloh but I didn't remember Elnora's name but I told her I love her.

She called Brian Kenyon, my instructor at Florida School of Preaching and he mentioned there was a virus going around at school and maybe that was why I was sick. I finally settled down and fell sleep, Elnora said she had just nodded off and awoke suddenly thinking she needed to take me to the hospital right away. She woke me up and asked me to get dressed but I wouldn't go to the hospital on my own behalf so she said she was in pain, needed to go the emergency room, and I agreed to go to help her. The next few days were a blur to me. Elnora told me about the following events. We had just moved here but became friends with Trina and her son Stephen, our next-door neighbors. Elnora called Trina at about 2:00 a.m. explaining she needed to take me to the ER and asking if Kenny could stay at their house. According to Elnora, waking Kenny and explaining to him she had to take me to the hospital was hard. Kenny became frightened and tearful but helped her get me into the car and strapped me in. Kenny was stressed and didn't want me to leave him. His mother and stepmother had both died in the hospital and he was still grieving those losses. Considering all the tragedies he had experienced so young there is no doubt the thoughts that likely were going through his mind. Elnora knew something was seriously wrong and had to convince Kenny to let her take me to the hospital, promising to come back and give him an update as soon as possible.

Bartow Memorial Hospital was about 15 minutes from our home. Elnora pulled up and had to find a wheelchair to put me in and somehow got me out of her vehicle and using the damaged wheelchair, half dragging, half pulling me into the Emergency Room. Immediately the staff began to yell at her asking why she waited so long to bring me in. She replied she thought I had a virus and she was just able to get me in and the staff recognizing my condition responded they thought I was going into a diabetic coma. Elnora responded that I was not diabetic. Elnora said it seems as if every doctor that was there that night was working on me. She said they thought I was overdosing on drugs. She explained to them that I didn't do drugs nor did I even take aspirin. She said I had just gotten out of the Army in June. The doctors assured her that I was a diabetic and would have gone into a coma had she waited longer. I was told by her and the doctors later that a normal reading for diabetic was between 70 to 120. My sugar leveling was 1936. The doctors told Elnora that they did not know how I was still functioning, they said if I survived throughout the night, I would be blind and on dialysis.

Elnora left the hospital about 6 that morning so she could be home when Kenny got ready for school. He was relieved to see her but confused and concerned, she couldn't give him much information since the doctors were uncertain if or how much I would recover. She had insisted I make a copy of my medical records before I processed out of the Army and even though she no longer worked at the post office, she had not resigned so she still had health insurance and was able to add me as a dependent. She began to peruse my medical records and was astonished to see notes stating I complained of frequent thirst and urination, blurred vision, and my mother had died of a heart attack at age 49, related to diabetes. I was likely diabetic for many years yet the Army hadn't followed up and this could have been the outcome of their negligence.

She called Brian back updating him of my status and after sending Kenny off to school, she returned to the hospital with my medical records in case they would give the doctors some insight into my condition. When she walked into the hospital, she was greeted by the preacher, John Griffis and Larry Lloyd and John Faneuf, Elders of the North Jackson Church of Christ in Bartow, a nearby church Brian belonged to and that we had visited. They prayed with us and assured her they were in our corner. This was an understatement. Later that day Elnora was told the ladies of the church had planned delicious meals for our family for weeks and their overall support was invaluable. We had planned to place membership with them that Sunday but because Kenny was being discharged that day, we didn't have the opportunity to attend services. This church and others in the area as well as the Florida School of Preaching were so kind and giving at a time when we didn't know where to turn. They were such a blessing to our family.

I stayed in ICU for 4 days and another day in the hospital. I was released with a slew of prescriptions and instructions on a Sunday morning, when they finally got my reading down to 500, which is well above stroke level.

That next day was to be Elnora's first day at Publix but she had to call in and request that her beginning date be extended as she took me to the Tampa Veterans Administration Hospital where the staff worked diligently to fill prescriptions, give us Diabetic Education, and assist with things I would need to start this new chapter in my life. We all had to adjust to my new way of living as a diabetic. I had to take three insulin shots a day. I thought it would be very difficult for me because I hated needles. About a week later I returned to school to continue my studies. It took some time for all of us to get used to this new lifestyle. I always had to check my reading before every meal and give myself enough insulin for what I was about to eat.

The Veterans Administration assisted me in filing a claim for disability and because we had the medical records to show evidence of me probably having diabetes while on active duty, they did not try to deny this claim. My diabetes was initially rated at 20% but elevated to 60%. This improved our financial and living situation greatly because most of my medicines were provided by the VA and we could afford healthier foods that were necessary for my condition.

While recovering from my hospitalization and regaining my strength, I let Kenny's dog Shiloh out in the backyard to run around. It was a beautiful fall day and he enjoyed being outside. About an hour later I remembered the fence had holes, still feeling weak I rushed to the back door and panicked realizing that Shiloh had gotten out of the fence. I jumped in the car and drove around the block a couple of times looking for him. Elnora came home to take me to my doctor's appointment and I told her what had happened. She said that we would look for him once we returned from the doctor's appointment. We saw a neighbor and told her Shiloh had escaped and asked her to let us know if she saw him. When we returned home, she informed us Shiloh had been hit by a car. When Kenny came home, we told him and he cried for hours. I was still weak and not sure what to do. One of our neighbors went and picked Shiloh up and brought him to our house. Kenny started crying again,

Shiloh had become his best friend and constant companion when he was grieving. He spent many hours with him each day and taught him several tricks. I convinced Elnora that we should get him another dog so she contacted the ASPCA in Lackland. Kenny and I chose a newborn puppy, we had to wait couple of weeks to pick him up and when Elnora saw him, she decided he should be named Midnight. He was jet black and it reminded her of the poem, "The Creation" by James Weldon Johnson. The line was "Blacker than a hundred midnights down in a Cypress Swamp." When we were finally able to bring Midnight home, he stayed in Kenny's room and he came out when Kenny came out. He slept at the bottom of Kenny's bed for years.

CHAPTER 20

A BASKETBALL STAR EMERGES

Basketball season started at the local recreation department in Lakeland. Even though I was still attending school and recovering I was still at every practice. Kenny was maybe now 5'7". The coach right away saw the potential in Kenny. He was the best player on the team. Right the way the coach and the team depended on him to do everything and he didn't let them down. He did most of the scoring, rebounding, and even handling the ball when the other teammates could not. He was once again the tallest player on his team. I talked to the coach on several occasions.

After about three games. Kenny's coach called asking if I would coach the team because he had to take care of some business out of town. I told him I had just been released from the hospital and was recuperating. He said I should "do it for the kids." The coach had an assistant and I asked why the assistant couldn't take over, his response was that the assistant didn't know anything about basketball. I told him I would do it only if he informed the recreation department and his assistant coach, he did and I became the new coach. Our team was mediocre. Once again Kenny was the only one on the team that other teams had to be concerned about. Therefore, he did well but if your opponent knows that there was only one good player on the whole team, they are going to target that one player. That year they were eliminated in the first round. Kenny was second in scoring and second in rebounding. I felt he was cheated out of the MVP award, it was given to a kid that was older and his last year playing in that league. The runner up MVP was given to a kid on the same team as the MVP who averaged nine points a game. Kenny averaged 20 points that year and 15 rebounds yet received no award. At the end of the season, the players are ranked by stats. Kenny was ranked fifth overall in the 17-year-old and under league. Some of the fans were angry and said I should have said something. I realize I was in a biased city. The discrimination was further evidence when the referees gave my team unfavorable calls and if I questioned the referees, they threatened to throw me out of the game. They couldn't deny him of his spot on the All-Star Team which was coached by the league champions' coaches, brothers whose last name was Hunt. They had dominated the league for years. He played well with the MVP of the league and they won a couple of games then were beaten. The team that put them out was playing rough. They could not stop Kenny from scoring so they fouled him hard repeatedly, throwing him to the floor on several occasions. I was upset but the coaches did not seem to care about the hard fouls. I asked them to take him out of the game not wanting him to get seriously hurt. They had a draft every year before the season started. I knew if I could get a ball handler and another shooter, I could have a winning team.

The summer started and I was out of school for the summer. I worked diligently to keep in contact with his grandparents in Germany. It had been five years since the last time they saw Kenny. I learned German so that I could talk to them for him. Kenny who once spoke German fluently but when he started going to school with Americans he stopped. I decided to take him to Germany to see his grandparents in 2002.

We began planning our trip to Germany. It would be the first time I would have to speak primarily German. When we got there, his grandparents picked us up at the Bremen Airport and drove us to their house about an hour away. We had a wonderful time there, also had a chance to visit his aunts and uncles. We spent 10 days there and when we arrived back home Kenny had grown two inches. He now stood at 5'8". We know this because Elnora was the first one to point it out. As soon as she saw Kenny and commented he went to Germany shorter than her and came back taller.

The recreation department had it's draft in September. I was excited because this time I would be at the draft and choose the players that I wanted. The assistant coach tried to take over as the head coach but because he didn't have a kid on the team and I did, I remained as the head coach. As I watched the players doing the workouts, I noticed two guards that I wanted. I had to make a decision which one to take in the first round because one of the teams might get one of them. I chose Christian in the first round and was hoping that Oliver, the other guard would still be available in the second. I was afraid that he was going to be gone. When the second round began, he was still available and I had the third pick. The first and the second coaches chose other players. The third pick I chose Oliver and I knew then I would have a pretty good team with two ball handlers besides Kenny. Now I was in need of another big man to place alongside Kenny. I was sure the one that I had been watching would be gone. However, the third round came around and he was still there and I picked Brandon in the third round. Before the season began, we were supposed to call the parents and introduce ourselves as their sons' coaches. All the parents were very nice. When I called Brandon's parents they were surprised because they knew the Hunts and they had promised them they would draft Brandon. Brandon's mom told me later that they lied to her saying that he was gone in the first round and they could not get him. I told his parents that I picked him in the third round. I was not supposed to do it but I took a chance and did. I had an unofficial first practice with my new team because practice had not started according to the schedule and I saw the potential of my squad, we had a really good team.

October was the official start date of the season. We tried to practice as much each week as we could. It was hard at times to find a facility to have practice. Thanks to Jeff who had accepted his role as an assistant talking to his church, we were allowed to use their church gym. Some of the parents also got in contact with friends who had access to gyms and they allowed us to use their facilities. It was not always a great gym, but it was better than nothing. Right away we came out the gate winning our first five games with no problem. The teams realized that we were going to be a hard team to beat. The defending champions coached by the Hunt brothers were no match for our team. Lead by Kenny doing the scoring and rebounding, Christian and Oliver handling the ball bringing it up the court. and scoring as well our team was complete! The addition of these players freed Kenny to go down in the post and he was unstoppable, it got to the point where he could score at will. We defeated the defending champions coached by the Hunts twice during the season. The only thing that really slowed us down was that Christian and Oliver could not always be on the court at the same time. There was a rule that every player had to play a certain amount of time each game. Everything changed with how I was talked to and by the coaches and even the referees treated us differently, we had earned their respect. They tried everything they could to stop Kenny and everything failed, he was just so much better and taller. They double teamed him and sometime triple teamed him but it didn't matter, Kenny would find the open player and they scored. The other big man was Brandon, he started playing really well after a few games into the season. He rebounded the ball well especially if Kenny had to come out of the game to rest.

At last, we had won the league championship with a perfect season 13-0. Heading into the playoffs we were the favorite to win it all. Our team dominated the regular season and we started the playoffs the same way. There were some games where we blew the teams out from the beginning of the game. There were games where Kenny didn't play the third and fourth quarter because we were so far ahead. We became even more dominant in the playoff because I could play Christian and Oliver with Kenny and Brandon on the court at the same time as long as we needed them on the court. The rule that everyone had to play a certain amount of time did not apply in the playoffs. We made it to championship still undefeated. The Hunt's team made it to the championship with only two losses during the regular season. The losses they suffered were when they played us so our team played the Hunt's for the championship. We dominated most of the game. The Hunts tried to be tricky after they had tried everything they could and could not slow my team down. They coached their players to try and get Kenny to foul them. They would jump into Kenny and fall down and the referee would call a foul on Kenny. They had a play called, "The Kenny Sandwich" where they would all crowd Kenny, making contact with him, hoping successfully that Kenny would be called for a foul. (We learned this because many of the players were friends and the other team joked about how they would beat us using "The Kenny Sandwich.") We could see that this was something they had worked on in practice because they got Kenny in foul trouble and I had to take in him out of the game midway through the third. Luckily Christian, Oliver, and Brandon were able to hold onto a slight lead to get us into the fourth and starting the final quarter with a 10-point lead, I held Kenny on the bench for the first two minutes. Sending him back into the game, I told Kenny to be smart, don't hold your arms out at all because the players were running into his arms and falling and he was getting fouls called against him. I told him if they got close to him just hold his arms straight up in the air. Those final minutes seemed to take forever. With Kenny back in the game the lead increased to 15 points and they cruised to the win. This team had gone from fifth place the previous year to champions. It was sad that the coaches did not shake our hands and congratulate us on the win nor did their players. They hid in the locker room to avoid us.

Elnora had seen this terrible sportsmanship by the coaches and players so she had the idea to go outside and wait for them in the parking lot. As the Hunts exited the gym, she walked up to them and asked if they knew what we put on "The Kenny Sandwich?" They acted like they didn't know what she was talking about but she was not to be denied or deterred, her answer: "Hunts Ketchup!" She walked away triumphantly. She had managed basketball teams in high school and played in the Air Force so seeing grown men acting like children really made her angry, she wouldn't let them get away with being spoiled sports.

At the end of the season the recreation department staff had always given an MVP. They had given it the previous season. However, they told me they were not going to give an MVP for the league because we were already getting city championship trophies so they did not need to give an MVP trophy. I told them they weren't planning to give the MVP because it would have to be awarded to my son. I was not going to let them cheat him out of the trophy that he had won. They had cheated him the year before and they were not going to do it again. They had a ceremony and they gave him the MVP trophy.

Since my team won the regular season automatically that made me the coach for the all-star team which gave me the ability to pick my team. I was fair I didn't pick my whole team but I could have. I decided to be fair, my top four were the best players in the league so I chose Kenny, Christian, Oliver and Brandon. I selected the remaining players from other teams. One of the parents didn't like me being the coach because she was used to the Hunts coaching her son and the All-Star team. She brought her son to one practice, got upset and took him home saying her son will not be coming back. That was not a problem, I just added another one of my players. Brandon's parents, Judy and Randy Hulcher, who in the beginning were surprised when I called and told Judy that Brandon was on my team because they wanted their son to be on the Hunt's team. The Hulcher's later told me that they were glad that Brandon was on my team. This family became some of our closest friends in Lakeland.

We cruised through the All-Star tournament the same way we did with the regular season and the championship tournament. Kenny, Christian and Oliver were dominant. We got to an early lead in several games in the tournament that Kenny did not play but two quarters in most of the games. One game Oliver and Christian got into foul trouble, we had a large lead and I had taken Kenny out. Since we had no other ballhandler I had to put Kenny back in to play point guard and bring the ball up the court. I told him not to try and score, just pass the ball to his teammates. The second time Kenny brought the ball up court no one was open so Kenny shot and scored. The coaching staff from the other team got mad at me saying we were trying to run the score up on them. I could have because teams tried to do it to our team the previous year but I chose not to be like those coaches. We made it to the championship game with no problem but the team we had beaten in the second round made it to the championship game because it was double elimination tournament.

The championship game was played in TD Waterhouse in Orlando, the home of the Orlando Magic. I thought it would be an easy game because we had beaten them by 15 points before and could have beaten them by more. Much to my surprise it was a struggle, possibly because of the awe of playing in TDY Waterhouse. Our team was not playing well, they were missing shots, and their defense was not good. I was trying to get them to calm down and we went into halftime losing by 5 points. I was so angry I talked the whole halftime, they didn't even get to warm up. I tried to calm them down by telling them they could play better and they had already beaten this team. The second half they were a different team. They returned and became the dominant team they were throughout the season. Kenny was so dominant he had 25 points and 26 rebounds. My team and I had won the city and county championship as well as the All Star team tournament championship. We were also undefeated in the county tournament as well. I know the Hunt brothers were glad to see us go.

Our Recreation League team that year was amazing. We all became like an extended family. Since we were not from the area, the families embraced us, inviting us to their homes for meals and treated us well. The Colbert family invited us to Thanksgiving dinner one year where we had our first fried turkey. We enjoyed having the team to visit, it was great feeling appreciated and we celebrated by having a banquet where each of our players received a trophy emphasizing their unique strength and value to the team. We've stayed in contact with many of these families for over 20 years.

CHAPTER 21

In May 2003 I graduated from the Florida School of Preaching and we moved back to my hometown. Kenny entered the 7th grade at Bonaire Middle School, he was 6'1". I visited Warner Robins High School, my alma mater. The principle and I had attended school there together in the 1980's. He asked if I had any kids and I told him yes. He then asked did my son play any sports. I told him, yes, he plays basketball. He told me that same day bring my son over to meet the high school basketball coach. I told him he is just in the seventh grade and he said it didn't matter. Once Kenny got out of school and came home, I told him the head high school basketball coach wanted to meet him. Kenny was just as surprised as I was since he was only in middle school. We went to the school and they told us that the coach was at the football game because he was coaching ninth grade football. Coach Chip Malone was the head basketball coach, we walked up to him and he just started smiling. He introduced himself and we talked for a few minutes. We could see right away that he had big plans for Kenny. Kenny started his first season as a basketball player at Bonaire Middle School.

Once again Kenny was dominant on the boards and shooting. He was the tallest on his team. This resulted in him playing out of his natural position which was a guard. He was doing it all. It did not take long for the rest of the schools in county to hear about his dominant playing. Bonaire Middle School didn't go far in the playoffs because once again he had little to no help. He continued being the best player in the league. The majority of the time he was unstoppable.

There was a lack of talent and experience on his team so they were not able to always get the win. Kenny was the talk of the city and of the Middle School. At the end of the season, he was awarded the MVP. This was his third MVP. His future looked bright and there would be many more MVPs to come

Kenny heard from some of his friends about tryouts for an AAU. Kenny showed up and the coach was the father one of his teammates at Bonaire Middle. It did not take long to figure that the coach already had his favorites and my son happened not to be one of them. Kenny had been dominating in the practices. The day before the first game the coach announced his starters and Kenny was not one of them. Kenny and I were both very upset because Kenny was clearly the best player on the team. Kenny did not grow up in Warner Robins with the other kids on the team so the coach started the kids he already knew, he was also friends with their parents. The assistant coach happened to be my cousin and asked me not to let Kenny quit because he can earn a starting position. The assistant coach's son was starting and my son was better than his son as well. I told the coach it is up to Kenny because I didn't believe Kenny should be coming off the bench. When we got home. I talked to Kenny and told him to come off the bench the first game and once he gets in the game, play like we know he can and he will continue to be dominant. We got to the game and once the starters walked on the floor a lot of the fans that had seen Kenny play were talking and very surprised that Kenny was not a starter.

The first two minutes of the game Kenny's team were doing poorly, they were getting blown out. Kenny entered the game and right away things started changing and they started scoring. The coach now realized the decision not to start Kenny was a mistake. Kenny didn't come off the floor the rest of the game and they won. I suspect the coach was afraid to try and bench Kenny because everyone saw what Kenny could do and how the other players played off him. Kenny was also a good passer. By this point Kenny realized that he could basically score when he wanted. He didn't mind sharing the ball. They had a pretty good AAU season.

Since Kenny was taller than most of the students in seventh & eighth grade the football coach convinced him come out and play for him on the eighth grade football team. The coach said they would throw the ball a lot to him because he was always taller than the cornerbacks that were trying to guard him. The coach did not keep his promise and the team threw the ball that season only three times. Coach Malone heard Kenny was playing football and he was angry. He told that coach not to play Kenny because he did not want him to get hurt, the coach played him anyway but he made sure he did get hurt.

Middle School basketball season started again and this time Kenny and his team at Bonaire were playing well. That season they had won the first four games. Kenny had started to get some help from his teammates and they finished the season with a good record. They were going into the playoffs with the best record and was a favorite to win the championship. One of the Middle School teams that was not as good the previous season so coach needed to improve or get fired so he did some illegal recruiting. A kid that was actually too old to play in the eighth because he was supposed to be in the ninth grade. He was also academically ineligible to play. He left one middle school and went to another one in the same county. If he was ineligible to play at one school, he was ineligible in all the schools.

Kenny and his team beat them the first time even though they had that ineligible player. He was actually taller than Kenny. Kenny and his team went into playoffs with the best record and had to play that team with the ineligible player which had the 4th best record.

The game started horribly for Bonaire Middle. The first two minutes of the game our team was crippled by turnovers. They were unable to get the back across the court and couldn't get the ball into Kenny's hands. After falling behind by ten points in the first three minutes of the game, the coach called a timeout and benched his starters. When this happened, the other team is pulled far away in scoring and the starters did not come back in the game in the first quarter. The coach failed to put the starters in at the beginning of the second quarter and Bonaire is falling further and further behind. At halftime, the players were warming up and I went to the court to talk to Kenny, suggesting to Kenny what he could do to help get the ball across the court. Kenny told me that he didn't think the coach was going to put them back in the game. I told Kenny if the third quarter started and he was still on the bench, I was going to get him and take him home. The coach came out of the dressing room and I think he heard me, when that quarter started Kenny was the only starter put back into the game. He went into the game and his team was losing by 30. Since the second squad guards could not get the ball over the court either. Kenny would go get the ball and bring the ball up the court himself. He came back into the game dominating and they could not stop him. When the game came to an end Kenny and his team were eliminated. Kenny did his best to give them a chance to win the game. He had about 26 points and they lost by 15 points when they were down by 30 when Kenny came back into the game. The coach threw that game away. He took the team's starters out of the game because they were losing by 10 points early on and didn't put them back in. In the end, it was one of the worst seasons for Bonaire Middle school.

When Kenny was in middle school, we were told we were zoned for Warner Robins High School but about a month before he was to enter high school, we were told that was erroneous and he would go to a different school. We didn't like that so I took a job as a paraprofessional in the school system since school employees here could send their children to any school in the district. We later bought a house in the Warner Robins High School zone so that Kenny would go to my alma mater and play for Coach Malone. He would become a Warner Robins Demon.

The summer before his freshmen year we heard about a sports camp in Suwanee, a town north of Atlanta. They offered a shooting lab where they taught skills to help with many aspects of the game. Kenny was already a "true" three point shooter but we decided to see what this clinic could offer. He was filmed shooting the ball and his shot was slowed down and analyzed by the staff, specifically showing the placement of his feet, his arms, stance, and how his shot looked as it glided toward the basket. This amazing staff taught Kenny how to perfect his shot, maximizing the motion and capitalizing the opportunity for it to be a more successful basket.

Kenny was spotlighted in a Prep Star Magazine where he was ranked in the top 50 players in Georgia for his projected high school graduation class. They covered and posted the rating results to this magazine. There was a camp where he was invited to participate with other players in his age group so that they would be ranked in the magazine. Kenny played well but he did not stand out. Going into the last game, I told Kenny he had to do something outstanding to get the attention of the staff they were rating the players. Kenny went onto the court, stole the ball and one player stood between him and the goal at the other end of the court. This player happed to be 6'7" and Kenny at the time was 6'2". I was sitting down and trying to watch the game but everyone around me stood up. They began laughing and clapping, I stood up to see what was happening and Kenny was standing over the taller player who was laying on the floor. Evidently, he didn't think Kenny would dunk on him. Kenny posterized this player and it got the attention of the staff.

CHAPTER 22

BEGINNING HIS HIGH SCHOOL CAREER

Coach Malone contacted me and told me he wanted Kenny to go to the summer camp with the varsity and junior varsity squads. The first day of the camp they had the varsity scrimmaging against the junior varsity. Kenny was scoring on all the varsity squad members with ease. He was the only one doing the scoring for the junior varsity. All the players on both squads were surprised. The second practice that afternoon Kenny and I walked in the gym. Coached Malone came over to me and told me that he had moved Kenny to the varsity squad.

This is the first time Kenny ever played with such a talented squad. During the second practice they were doing one on one drills. The varsity squad did not want to go up against Kenny, they were afraid he would embarrass them and he did most of the time. This was also the first time he was not the tallest player on his team. They had one week of practice in Warner Robins. The second week they traveled to Tallahassee, Florida to compete in a tournament. They played three games, winning two and losing one. Kenny played well when he got on the floor. At the end of the camp Coach Malone told the whole team that he was surprised at the way that Kenny played and he expected Kenny to play a major role in the team success in the upcoming season and in the future.

Just before the season began, they held tryouts for the both teams. Kenny participated in the tryouts. I thought Kenny had nothing to worry about but Kenny was not sure because the coach had him out there with the players that were trying to make the team. When the team list was posted, Kenny's name appeared with the varsity squad. Some of the junior varsity players were mad because Kenny jumped ahead of all them. Some the players on the junior squad were playing their second year with the junior varsity team.

The season started and because a lot of the basketball players were playing football, they only had seven players on the varsity squad. The first two preseason games they played with six players and one junior varsity player was on the bench just in case they needed another player. The preseason game was against Perry High. Kenny was once again playing out of his natural position as a point or shooting guard. Warner Robins had a very good point and a shooting guard named Pierre and Kenny Willis, so Kenny started at the center position. It was a close game and we thought the game was over. I was trying to beat the crowd out the door and I left the stands so I missed Kenny rebounding the ball with a few second left in the game. He got fouled and went to the free-throw line, making both shots sending the game into overtime. One of the players fouled out. The player they had on the bench came into the game. Then Kenny fouled out and they had to finish the game with only four players. The third preseason game the football players had joined the team.

Once all the football players joined the team Kenny came off the bench the rest of the season. There were times where he didn't get that many minutes his first season. Their team made it to the Sweet 16 in the state tournament before being eliminated. In the playoffs Kenny got more playing time because in one game the junior that was playing the small forward could not guard a 6'7" player. This player scored most of their points the first half of the game. The second half Kenny entered the game to guard that player. Kenny was so excited to get in the game that he was going to do everything in his power to stay on the floor. Kenny was about 6' 2" and Kenny shut this player down. Kenny frustrated him so much he was not playing well and they took him out of the game. Kenny also replaced the junior who was originally the starter because this player had become afraid to shoot because he had some missed shots, Kenny was not afraid to shoot. At the end of the season Kenny had accumulated a lot of playing time that year so he qualified for a letterman jacket. He was the only ninth grader that season playing on the varsity squad in the county and the first freshman to receive a letterman jacket.

CHAPTER 23

OFFSEASON

His freshman year was a humbling experience. He had never spent so much time on the bench in a basketball game since he started playing when he was five years old. He accepted his role on the bench and was always ready to play when called upon. Never complaining, he just went with the program. The team had their two weeks summer practice and he played better that summer because he was more familiar with the players and he had proven himself to the older teammates who now trusted and respected him and his ability to play.

During the summer they could only participate in AAU because the majority of the time when school was in session even if basketball season was over, they weren't allowed to play until a certain time. Kenny heard about an AAU team holding tryouts in Macon. I went to the practice with him. Kenny and I got there early and we were going through some shooting drills. Players came into the gym and joined us in our drills. Coach Melvin Flowers saw us and asked me to coach the 15-and under team. I was always eager to help and to create opportunities for Kenny and other players who really wanted to learn. That year we had a good season qualifying our first year for the national tournament that was hosted at Disney World of Sports in Orlando. Unfortunately, we were unable to raise the money to finance our trip so we were not able to go that summer.

Warner Robins High School hosted the tryouts for the basketball team in October. This time Kenny did not have to try out, he had earned his spot on this team. Being the dedicated player that he was, he still was out there with the players that were trying out. When the list was posted no one was surprised to see Kenny on the list with the varsity squad.

The season went well, they won the regional title for the second year in the row. That season Kenny started at the power forward. He really contributed to the overall team success. He averaged about 15 points that season and the team made it to the Elite Eight in the state tournament. To make it this far, they had to play against a team that was the favorite to win the state. They were ranked in the top three in the state. With this fact, I am not sure why they had to come play at our arena. They had brothers on that team who were each at least seven feet tall. Coach Malone decided not turn on the air conditioner in the gym during this game. Everyone was upset because it was very hot in the gym, until we found out the reason behind this strategy. This team was used to playing in air-conditioned buildings. Coach Malone was a true genius, funny, smart, and he was trying to create an edge. He also played a zone instead of man to man. He figured out the 7-footers did not like getting hit so they were hitting them often. After a short time, these tall athletes would no longer go down in the post under the basket so they were not able to get rebounds or easy shots. They started shooting from the outside. They were decent outside shooters but this strategy created mismatches to their disadvantage. We shocked this team and many that did not give us a chance of winning this game. These players were much softer than our inner-city players and with no air conditioning and hard fouling, we were able to stay close and pull out the win at the end. These opponents were so embarrassed they did not even shake hands with our team. One player that tried being a good sport and shaking hands and congratulating our team but was yelled at by his teammates and their coaches. This was probably the first time that Warner Robins Boys basketball team had ever made it to the Elite Eight. Our team lost in the next round and this would be the end of a great run for Kenny and his teammates because every player on the varsity squad graduated. Kenny entered his junior year realizing he would be a part of a rebuilding team for the next two years.

There were several die heart fans from Warner Robins High and many supported all of the sports teams. This was the oldest school in city. When the season started, a group of fans who had graduated from Warner Robins in the 1960s and they sat at the top of the bleacher. This group would be at almost every game and my wife and I were honored that they let us sit with them. The gym would get packed but it never felt crowded because it was like family. When Kenny would get a hot streak, which was often, you could hear the crowd joyfully shouting, "It's Flu Season!" and the chant would take off like wildfire.

During the summer Kenny once again looked around to see what AAU team he would play with. He checked out several teams before we decided to try once again at coaching and starting our own team. This time I met the person that took over as the Director of the Perry Recreation Center, a small city in our county. He agreed to let us use his facility to practice and host our games and tournaments. We had a few players from Warner Robins and a few players from Perry. It was also the second time he got a chance to play with his cousin, Jared (JJ). They had always played against each other in middle school because they lived in different cities and school zones. Kenny was either taller or they were the same height. Once again we qualified for the national tournament at the end of the summer in Florida but we were unable to raise the money to pay for the trip and the hotel.

CHAPTER 24

REBUILDING SEASON

Kenny entered the 11th grade not sure of what kind of team he would be playing for. To his surprise a lot of players that were not getting that much playing time in the schools that they had attended last season found a loophole in the Board of Education policy for changing schools. The Houston of County Board of Education passed a bill that if a student was attending a school that didn't do well on the exit examination, they could transfer to a school that performed well. Several players used this policy to come to Warner Robins High since all the players had graduated except Kenny. Jared Fluellen Jr. (JJ), who he had always competed against Kenny also came to Warner Robins High School. Several other players came from across town and made the team. It looked like we could possibly have a good season.

Everyone was assuming that Kenny was going to lead this team since he was the only player returning from the two successful previous years. The first game did not go so well for him. Kenny's cousin did well and out shined Kenny. JJ had about 20 pts and Kenny had 12. Kenny was very upset with himself. The pressure was getting to him. That night we had a long discussion and he was so upset and frustrated he said he was considering not playing anymore. I talked to him and told him it was just one game. I convinced him to calm down and relax, reminding him that he always faced challenges and overcame them and he would do the same thing this season.

The second game of the season some had started thinking that JJ was going to be the biggest scoring threat on the team but Kenny had other plans in mind. Just as I knew he would, Kenny played very well. He had 25 points the second game and his cousin had 10 points. The rest of the season Kenny got better and he became the player that Coach Malone knew he would become. They failed to make the state tournament for the first time in three seasons. Kenny led the team in scoring and rebounding. Although he had been scouted by Florida State's Head Coach since he was in the 10th grade when he entered the 11th grade the letters stopped coming. I went to their webpage and saw that they had signed several guards. At the end of the season Kenny won the MVP to go along with the two he had received at Bonaire Middle School.

Their two weeks of training for Warner Robins High School basketball summer camp was held locally for the first time because they cut the money for the summer camp. Kenny and I decided that we would try to get him on an AAU team in Atlanta because the teams in Atlanta had major sponsorships which enabled them to travel all summer. Kenny made the squad for a team there. That summer Kenny was gone most of the summer, traveling from camp to camp, state to state. He was averaging about 26 points a game. The college coaches were calling asking when Kenny would be home and they wanted to come and meet him. I told them that he is not heading home yet, he was on the road playing AAU in camps around the Southeast U.S. Many coaches told me that they were going to go see him various camps, this happened repeatedly all summer long. At the national tournament in Orlando, I watched some of the games. These coaches were lined up along the walls watching players. Kenny's scoring average went down to 16 points and 10 rebounds a game. It was weird after about two games fewer and fewer coaches were following him and attending his games. I never heard from these coaches again unless I contacted them. I didn't understand what the problem was. They all knew what he was capable of and looking at some of the stats of college players as well as some of the other recruits, some of them were not even averaging 16 points a game as Kenny was.

Two weeks before Kenny started his senior year in high school. He and I were contacting colleges. We set up a tryout with Jacksonville University. He had a good showing going through all the drills. He also played well during the scrimmage games. However, we did not hear from them. He had a tryout with Palm Beach Junior College in Florida. He had a good workout with this junior college as well. A week later the coach contacted Kenny and offered him the scholarship. Kenny decided not to take the scholarship because he wanted to be able to travel home while he was at college and this school was too far of a distance for a short visit home.

CHAPTER 25

KENNY'S SENIOR YEAR

Kenny began his senior year not knowing where he would be attending college or if he would receive a basketball scholarship. Limestone College in Gaffney, South Carolina and Paine College in Augusta, Georgia were interested in signing him. We had informed them that he would prefer to attend a Division 1 School and both of these schools were Division 2. They continued to pursue him by sending him letters. I contacted several Division 1 schools and several of them said they were coming to check out some of his games but they didn't. They even said good basketball players don't come out of Warner Robins, Georgia, noting that Warner Robins is known for their talented football players, not basketball players. I caught several Division 1 coaches being dishonest about their intent to see him. Several of them told me that no Division 1 scout was going to come and watch a losing team even if my son was as good as I said he was. Some of the Division 1 college coaches said they could not really evaluate Kenny as a guard which was his natural position because he was playing small forward or power forward at the high school. The only time Kenny actually had to bring the ball up the court and run the offensive was when the guards could not bring the ball across the court without turning it over. Kenny was an exceptional ball handler and talented at bringing the ball up the court, breaking the traps, giving the ball to the guard, and then going into the post. The coaches and scouts used this as an excuse why they didn't attend any of his games.

Kenny was having another great year. We had a few junior colleges to show up and scouted him. Some of the scouts came to the game and one particular scout told Kenny that the scouts needed to see more from him if he wanted a scholarship. That scout was in attendance and must have fired Kenny up before the game. He said Kenny needed to do more on both ends of the floor as if he was not playing hard enough. We all figured that Kenny would play well but we had no idea how well. Kenny was all over the floor shooting, rebounding, and playing defense. He made a three pointer the last few seconds on the clock going into halftime. Kenny started the second half the same way hitting three pointers and getting to the basket. They were playing against Colquitt County High School. Even though Kenny was playing well they were still losing because he had little help. The coach for the opposing team was concerned that Warner Robins would make a comeback and win the game because they could not stop Kenny. He was trying everything. He double teamed him and that did not work. Warner Robins came up short in the end in making a complete comeback, losing by a mere five points. After the game, the stat keeper came up to me and told me that Kenny had set a new school record for scoring in a single game. The record was about 30 points. Kenny had just scored 44 points. As of now, this single school scoring record still stands.

Once again Kenny's team failed to make the state playoffs. Kenny was named MVP for a second year in a row. He made All Middle Georgia First Team for second year in a row. He finished his high school career fifth on the all-time scoring list. Kenny averaged 22 points, eight rebounds, and five assists his senior year. The player who once held the single season scoring record heard about Kenny breaking his record and he attended some of the games before the season ended. Kellen Milner wanted to meet Kenny and they spoke after a game. He asked Kenny if he had ever considered playing basketball overseas. Kenny told him he had not thought about it.

Since none of the Division One school scouts attended any of Kenny's game and were no longer contacting him, Kenny decided to take some visits to two Division 2 schools. We first visited Limestone College. Gaffney is on the South Carolina/North Carolina state line, about seven hours from home. It would be difficult for us to visit him and watch his games, especially in the winter when it snowed and we would have to spend the night when we visited since it was so far away. We made a family visit to the school and Kenny scrimmaged with the team and played well. He was scoring on their starters with ease. After the workout, Kenny visited with the players. Elnora, Kenny and I met with the coaching staff. They told us as everyone saw the way Kenny played and he might not start but it would be hard to keep Kenny off the floor and that he would play a valuable role as freshman for their team if he signed with them. They offered him a full scholarship on the spot. Kenny said he wanted to think about it and there were some other schools he wanted to visit before making a decision.

Kenny's second visit was to Paine College. Paine is a part of the Historical Black College & University System

(HBCU) about two and a half hours from our home. The gym didn't have air conditioning but we liked the home town feel. It was within a few blocks of the Veterans Administration Hospital and the people there were really excited to meet us.

Some of the players were present and the some of the assistant coaches played in the scrimmage game with Kenny. Kenny once again did well. They could not stop him from scoring. The athletic director said he probably could not give him a full scholarship but the assistant coach that tried to guard Kenny during the scrimmage game stopped by and said he would take money from his baseball team to make sure they signed Kenny. The Athletic Director said he would do whatever he needed to do to sign Kenny to a scholarship. All of the coaches loved him and wanted him to sign with Paine. When we were in the car leaving the school, Kenny told us that he could not play at a school where the gym did not have air conditioning. The Athletic director had told us during our meeting with him that they were in process of building a new gym.

When signing day arrived Kenny and the family arrived at Warner Robins High School to sign with a college. Kenny signed his letter of intent to play for Limestone College Saints. Elnora made the comment Kenny went from the Warner Robins Demons to the Limestone College Saints.

CHAPTER 26

KENNY BEGINS HIS COLLEGE CAREER

Kenny was excited about starting his college career doing what he loves, playing basketball. When practice started Kenny was doing well with all the practice coaches telling him that he was doing a great job. Nothing prepared Kenny for what would happen next. The first game Kenny sat on the bench the whole game and the coaching staff said nothing. The following week everything was the same as before, he practiced as if he would be playing the next game. The second, third, and fourth games Kenny did not come off the bench. Kenny was very upset and he called me after talking with the coaching staff. He said the head coach told him that he would be redshirted this season. This was not what they had told us when we came for a visit so Kenny was ready to transfer and leave this school. I reminded him that he was on scholarship so he sat on the bench the whole season. They promised Kenny that he would start his sophomore year. He was allowed to practice with the team and travel with the teams but could play not in the games.

That summer Kenny decided to attend some overseas pro combines. He played well in these combines and the coordinator of these combines advertised that pro scouts would be at these camps and would be signing players on the spot. That did not happen, no players were signed. After attending several of these combines, we realized it was a money maker for the organizers. Some overseas agents noticed him and we learned that summer because Kenny's mother was German, he could play in Germany as a national player if he got their citizenship. We were always told in order for him to get his German citizenship he would have to serve in the German Army for a year. Kenny was not willing to do that when he turned 18 years old. We checked with the German consulate in Atlanta and they informed us that it was no longer a requirement to serve in the German Army to obtain his German citizenship. They informed us of the necessary paperwork in order for him to get his German Citizenship. Once all the paperwork was filled out, he received his German Citizenship as well as his German Passport. He did not get signed to an oversees team that summer.

Kenny returned to Limestone College for his sophomore year. This was the year the coaching staff had promised that Kenny would be a starter. Before the season started, the player that was supposed to be second string behind Kenny that season found some paperwork showing that a new player that had never practiced with the team had been put into the starting lineup. Kenny was bumped to the second string and the guy that was supposed to be second string was pushed to third string. He told Kenny about this paper and asked Kenny to go with him and confront the coaching staff. Kenny decided he would wait until practice started and he would prove that he deserved to start.

The season started and they were going to the practices and preseasons games. Kenny played well doing the preseason. The first game Kenny did not start, the player started instead. After a few games the new player continued to start the game instead of Kenny. I told Kenny not to worry about it, just outplay him in the practices and he will gain his starting position. Kenny told me that he was already outplaying the newer player in practices, yet at game time the coach would put in the new guy. I was able to go to a few games and thought if I had the chance to talk to the coach it might make a difference. One of the games I attended, the coach played Kenny but never put him in the starting roster. He would put him in with bench players so that he could not shine, however he made a mistake and put Kenny on the floor with four of the starters. Kenny came into the game, went down the court, and made a three pointer. He got back on defense, stole the ball, went down the court, and made a layup. The head coach immediately pulled Kenny out of the game. Not only did I get upset but other fans did also because it was clear he was trying to keep Kenny from outplaying the new guy.

After the game I tried to talked to the head coach and he told me he doesn't talk to parents during the season. I was at several games watching and hoping that Kenny would get more opportunities to prove that he deserved to start. I talked to the only coach that would talk to me, he wasn't the coach that recruited Kenny, asking him if the new guy was outplaying Kenny in practice. He confirmed what Kenny had told me that at every practice Kenny outplayed this teammate. At the next game the coach again put him in instead of Kenny. I did my research and talked to NCAA personnel and was informed that Kenny could ask for a transfer if he is not happy at a particular school. I talked to Kenny and he said the coach had assured him that he would get a lot of playing time the next game but that didn't happen.

The next day Kenny called me and asked for suggestions on what I thought he should do. I also had talked to a coach at Fort Valley State college that had tried to recruit Kenny earlier. He told me to tell Kenny he must not act like he was unsure if he really wanted to transfer. I told Kenny he must be serious and regardless of what the coach said, tell him he wanted to be released so he can transfer. Kenny called me and said he had spoken to the head coach and that this coach would probably call me. I didn't think he would actually call me after he would not talk to me before. Much to my surprise he did and asked if I knew that Kenny had asked for his release and I said yes, asking him the point of this call. He told me he doesn't have to release Kenny if he doesn't want to. Much to his surprise, I told him I had checked into and spoke with The NCAA compliance office and they had given me all the information and guidelines about transferring. I informed him I would report him to the NCAA compliance office if he didn't release Kenny. An hour later Kenny called me and told me that he has his release paperwork. This was a few weeks before the Christmas break.

Now that Kenny had paperwork to show that he was released from Limestone College, he could pursue other avenues for his educational and athletic endeavors. When Kenny came home for Christmas break, I informed him I had been in contact with the head coach at Fort Valley State College. This coach told me to have Kenny come to the practice once he is released and is home. Kenny showed up at several practices and was playing well. One day he called me from the practice and said that he was playing well but because his team was not playing well, the head coach would take him out. The coach began yelling at his team because of their lack of effort and I told Kenny to try and get back in the game. Kenny responded that he had tried and the head coach kept taking him out. I told Kenny not to worry, come home and we will try another school, not knowing what would happen.

I remembered that the head coach at Mercer University had been trying to recruit Kenny when he was in high school so I contacted the coaching staff and they told us to come to the school. After a tryout, the assistant coach told us he really liked Kenny but there were no scholarships available, that we would probably have to pay for Kenny's first semester, and then he would get picked up on scholarship. This was a Division One private school about 30 minutes from our home so we thought about it. My wife was recently graduated from Mercer. We went to the Admissions Office and were considering paying for his first year. I decided to pause this action and returned to talk to the assistant coach. This time the assistant coach told me the truth, stating that honestly Kenny was more likely not going to get picked up on a scholarship after his first semester because there were players that had already paid for a semester or two and they would be next in line to get a scholarship. We did not enroll him at Mercer because we couldn't afford to pay for several semesters at Mercer.

Our third school we decided to check out was Paine College. We contacted the athletic director at Paine College he told us to contact his assistant coach, Coach Link. We contacted Coach Link and he asked us to come to the school to work out with the team. We drove there expecting to see this new gym. Much to our surprise it was still the same old gym with no air conditioning. Later we found out from my wife's sister that Paine College had been promising to build a new gym since the 1960s. This was our last school. We also discovered that Kenny would have to sit out again. I contacted the NCAA Compliance Office and they informed me because he played a few minutes at Limestone College he could not play with two schools in the same year. He had to sit out the rest of that year and could start playing with the team the next year.

Kenny returned to Paine that Fall semester eligible to start playing with the team. He was now on a full scholarship. We didn't know until the season started that there were several players playing the same position as he was playing. Coaches seems to like to play the upper classmen first. Kenny got some playing time but he believed he deserved more and I did too after watching the other players. That was however not what the coach decided. At times we did not agree with his decisions when it came to the playing time given to Kenny during his first year with Paine. That season Kenny played well in several games. His highest scoring games were against Tuskegee and Clark where he scored that season was 19 points. With limited playing time he averaged 7 points a game that season.

That summer Kenny was not sure what to expect when he returned to Paine in the Fall. I decided to go to a couple of pro combines and tryouts with him. He was contacted by some NBA D-league teams about attending their tryouts and they also promised that players would get signed to contracts. As usual that was not the case. No one got signed, it was all just to make money for their particular team. He also tried out with more overseas showcases with no one getting signed at the end. The scouts at the NBA D-league and the overseas leagues said they liked the way he played. The evaluation sheets at the camps all stated that he was a good player and shooter, possessing a great court vision. However, no contract.

CHAPTER 27

BREAKOUT SEASON

Kenny returned in the Fall to start his junior year at Paine. Their first game that season was at a local high school. They finally had begun to build Paine college a new gym, starting once the previous season was completed.

Their first game in the new gym was against Stillman on January 5, 2013. That night Kenny missed his first two shots. I started to think this would not be a good game for him shooting the ball. Kenny would prove us all wrong Coach Malone had always stayed on his team about floor spacing and Kenny reflected on these lessons, it was if a light came on and he knew what he needed to do. Throughout the rest of his college and professional career, he remembered how instrumental the lessons Coach Malone taught him, finding the open space and balance for the floor. Kenny positioned himself and created open shots that enabled to score easily, christening the new gym at Paine. He did not miss many shots the rest of the night. Kenny led all scorers with 27 points, he shot 50% from behind the arc that night. There was nothing the Stillman players could do to stop him. When he was forced off the three-point line he drove to the basket and scored and when they fouled him, he made his free-throws. His next highest scoring game came when they played against Albany State when he scored 23 points. That season he averaged 10 points a game.

That summer Kenny and I spent most of his time in the offseason trying to improve every aspect of his game. Each summer previously he had made 300 shots a day. The offseason before his senior year at Paine he made a total of 500 shots a day. We spent many hours in the gym working on his speed, dribbling, and getting to the basket more. He also was in weight room lifting trying to build upper body strength. He was still hoping to catch the eye of a pro scout overseas or the NBA D-league. We sent highlight videos to coaches overseas as well as to NBA D-league. More of the overseas teams seemed to be interested than the NBA D-league. However, several D-league teams contacted him based on the information they had gotten from the previous overseas showcase and NBA D-league trying to invite him to their camps. We had become wise to their game, they were only trying to make money so we ignored their invitations.

In the fall of 2013 Kenny returned to Paine for his senior year. He started the preseason off strong. He scored 19 points in the first preseason game and 21 in the second, leading all scorers and ended the preseason averaging 14.7 points per game. His highest scoring game came when they played against Stillman College in which he scored 22 points. His second highest game of the season was when he played against his childhood friend who played with Fort Valley State University. It was a shootout between him and his best friend. Kenny led his team in scoring and Brandon led his team in scoring. Kenny scored 20 points in this game shooting 72% from behind the arc making five of seven three pointers. He averaged 13 points during the regular season and 12.6 points in the playoff that season. He shot 40% from behind the arc his senior year, the best of his college career.

He accumulated 66 assists, eight blocked shots, and 21 steals. He was named to the Southern Intercollegiate Athletic Conference (SIAC) post season team and was the MVP for the Lions following the 2013-14 season. He had the third highest average in the three-points percentage made in the SIAC.

His time at Paine was a great experience for him. He became close to many of the players, fans, staff, and community. Coach Link and his coaching staff were warm and supportive. Coach Link once remarked that Kenny could "shoot the paint off the ball." Athletic Director Tim Duncan and his family were equally supportive and our decision for Kenny to join that team and community was a good decision.

After the close of the season, he signed with an agent, Daryl Graham, to play basketball overseas. Thanks to the local newspaper in Augusta he was spotted by the Graham's mother, who lived there. Daryl was living in New York but Mrs. Graham read the article and told her son about the outstanding player at Paine. He asked her to go to the game and watch Kenny play and she said after seeing the game she went home the same night and told Daryl he needed to get to Georgia as soon as he could and sign Kenny to a contract. Daryl came home and their family invited us to dinner where we talked about the prospect of him representing Kenny. Daryl also represented his brother who was playing in Italy so it was such an easy decision so Kenny signed a contract for one year with his agent.

CHAPTER 28

KENNY STARTING HIS PROFESSIONAL CAREER

Kenny began his first professional contract to play overseas. He signed with BG Karlsruhe in Karlsruhe Germany for the 2014-15 season. It was an exciting time for him to continue playing the sport that he so loved. We drove him to the Atlanta Airport and said our goodbyes. This was the first time he would be flying by himself and being in Germany by himself. There was one American and a player from England who also was on his team. Kenny had dual citizenship so he was treated as a German. There were no restrictions on how much time he could play. This was not true with the American and the player from England. BG Karlsruhe played in the Bundesliga 2nd division.

That first season went well. They made it to the first round of the playoffs but were eliminated there. Kenny's highest scoring game came when he scored 30 points and led all scores as he helped his team to win the game. They won the first three games then they would lose one and then win one. He ended the season averaging nine points a game.

I think that summer, the most difficult skill Kenny had to add to his arsenal to make him a more complete player was dribbling. He was a decent ball handler but if he worked on this skillset he would become a double threat-scoring from the outside as well as driving to the basket. I noticed when he first arrived at Paine, his time was reduced if he was not making shots. We added 30 minutes of dribbling to each of his workout sessions. Kenny first saw this as just a time-consuming task. We created combination drills for dribbling such as through the legs and behind the back to enhance his ability to create separation between himself and the defender. Once these combinations were perfected, it would allow him to effectively create a better shot and get to the basket and would also keep the defender guessing what he was going to do. As a result, the defenders were not being able to stay in front of Kenny when he was playing overseas.

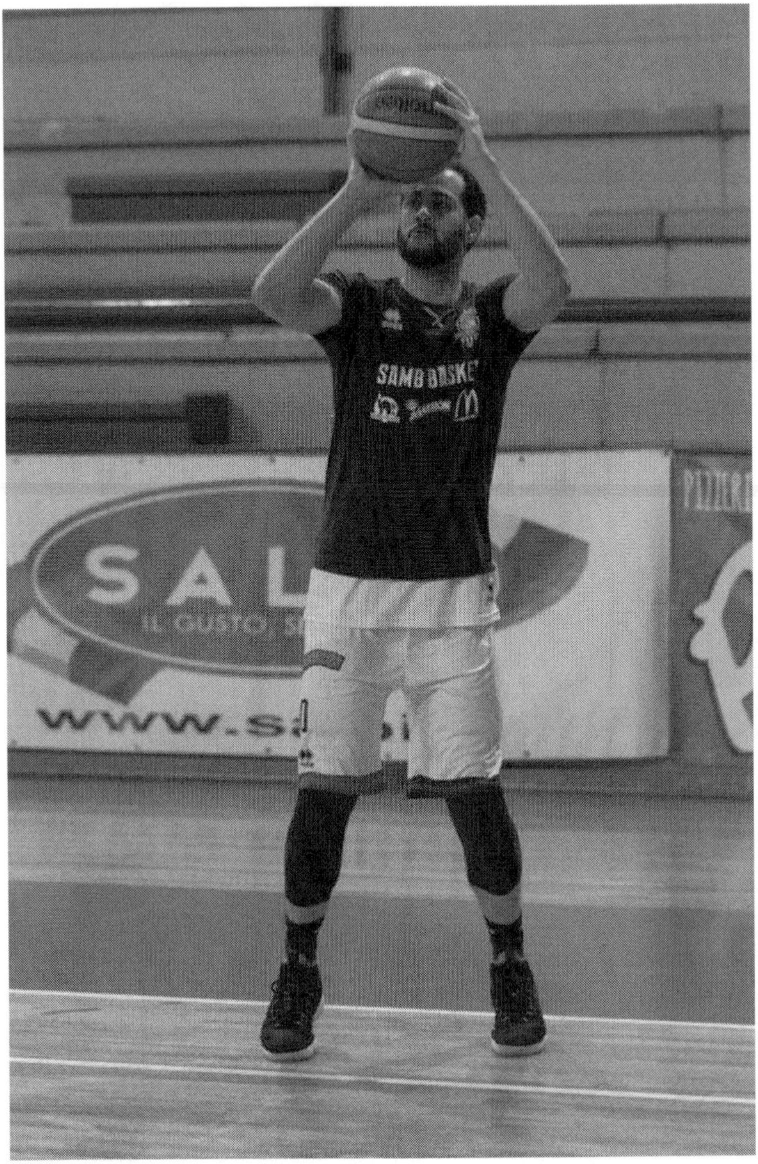
SAMB BASKET

Kenny would go on to play professional basketball for eight years overseas, seven season in Germany and in Iceland and Italy for half a season each. He played in First, Second, and Third Divisions Germany, First Division in Iceland, and Third Division in Italy. His highest scoring game in his career came when he was playing for Vilsbiburg in Italy when he had 37 points in the 2020 season. At the time they held seventh place in the division and they beat the team that was in first place in the division. He played his last season 2021-22 for Vilsbiburg, his highest scoring game that season came when scored 35 points. He finished the season averaging 20 points a game 46% from two-point range, 35% from the three point range, four rebounds, two assists, one steal, and made 77% of his free throws.

This indeed was a good basketball player that had the potential to be great but was overlooked by the Division1 colleges and the NBA simply because the city in which he played was known for football and not basketball. Two years ago he was working out with a player that had played in the NBA and the top division overseas and who had gone to a Division 1 college. The pro basketball trainers and coaches saw him working out with his friend. They liked the way he played and they told him that he was a good scorer and player. After the workouts they were talking like they were interested in him having a tryout but when they heard he went to a Division 2 school, they said they would contact him and he never heard from them again. It is unreal to me when a coach observes a player for hours and sees him playing against the Division 1 and NBA players and doing well against them and as soon as they realized he went to a Division 2 school they did not want to talk to him.

If the big universities and NBA teams knew what Kenny had to overcome with all the tragedies that he experienced early in life they too would come to the conclusion that Kenny is truly a special player. The things he had to overcome to accomplish more then those he played with in high school and college. Kenny was often complimented by players that played for the big universities, and players that played in the NBA about his work ethic. Kenny put in the time to achieve his dream of playing pro basketball. When Kenny was five years old, he told me that he was going to be a professional basketball player. Before his last season in 2021-22 he made 500 shots a day and still did other drills to improve on all aspects of his game.

Kenny became a coach after retiring from playing pro basketball overseas. He was the head coach for the boys' junior varsity and the assistant coach for the boys varsity team at Sanderson High School in Raleigh, North Carolina. Kenny and his wife Melissa are currently living in Nashville, North Carolina.

Kenny and I hope the writing of this book will inspire others to continue pursuing their goals even if the odds are stacked against them. This was a journey that started when he was five years old and there were pauses along the way. He never lost sight of his goal and neither should anyone who is desiring to achieve great things.

Kenny and I did not always agree on his training and what he could accomplish but I didn't give up on him and he didn't give up on me. I recognized it late but I did realize that Kenny had learned all that he could learn from me. By the time Kenny was in his final year of college our workout sessions no longer involved me coaching or instructing him. He had grown as a man and as a player. He was now instructing me on what he needed me to do to help him improve in every aspect of the game. My role changed from that as a trainer and coach to that of person being there to help assist him in any way I could.

The eight years he played professional basketball overseas he came home every summer during the offseason. We spent many hours together in the gym and he had absorbed so much knowledge from his many coaches that he was now teaching me. This is when I knew that I was just glad to be along for the ride. He taught me in the end and that enabled me to become a better coach. Who knew that his love of the game of basketball would expand to over twenty plus years.

I had the privilege of watching him coach his first high school squad. Seeing him in his new role as a coach brought many fun memories. I will always cherish times we spent practicing and enduring training sessions together. Kenny learning from me and I from him. I hope that you continue to strive in your role as coach with the same never quit attitude that you obtained as a player. I am sure if you have this same attitude you will succeed as coach as you did as a player.

His first season as a coach came to end. During this season he saw a lot of ups and downs. He had a young team. He had only one or two players that had ever played before.

Toward the end of the season everyone could see the improvement of the team. Kenny also had grown in developing his coaching style. His practice was based on his scheduled training for each section, they were detailed and broken down by periods and included skills training as well as conditioning.

The next season he decided not to coach. He took a break from coaching and took a state job. His new position is working with the Department of Motor Vehicles. He hopes to return to coaching someday.

He recently started individual training with young players. He plans to grow his clientele in personal training believing he can help a lot of young players make it to the next level and be successful in achieving their goals whether it be as a college or a professional basketball player. During his last three years of playing professionally Kenny acquired the skill of analyzing films from games so that he could this share knowledge with teammates and coaches to determine strengths and weaknesses. This was an important technique that helped create an edge for future games and assisting players in shifting their focus in areas in which they needed development.

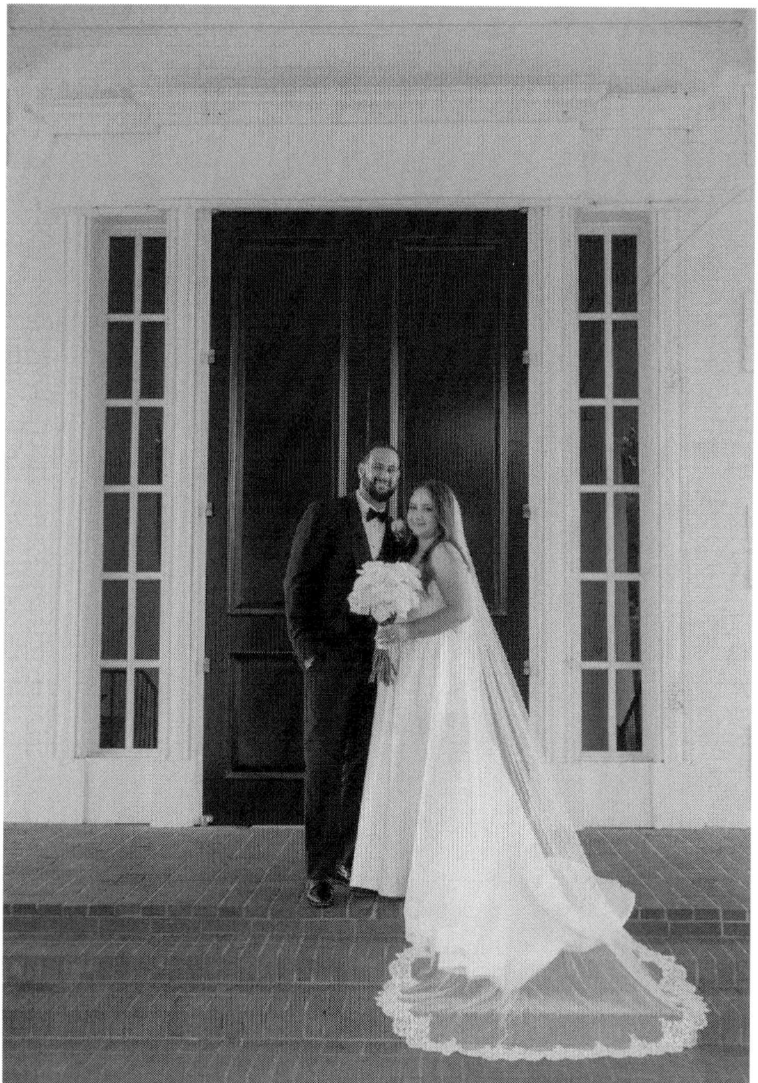

Made in the USA
Columbia, SC
20 February 2024